WHO AND WHERE
ARE THE REAL
CHRISTIANS?

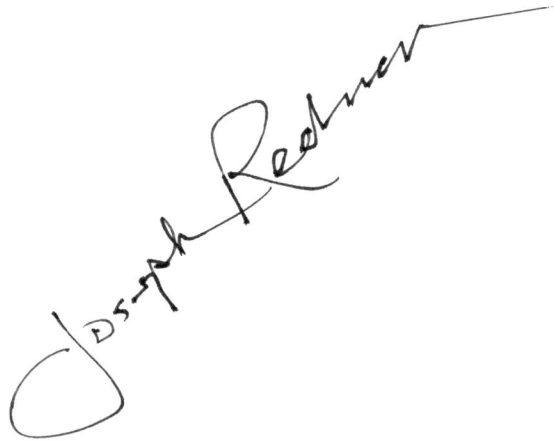

JOSEPH REDMAN

ISBN 979-8-88540-742-7 (paperback)
ISBN 979-8-88540-743-4 (digital)

Copyright © 2022 by Joseph Redman

All rights reserved. No part of this publication may be reproduced, distributed, or transmitted in any form or by any means, including photocopying, recording, or other electronic or mechanical methods without the prior written permission of the publisher. For permission requests, solicit the publisher via the address below.

Christian Faith Publishing
832 Park Avenue
Meadville, PA 16335
www.christianfaithpublishing.com

Scriptures marked ESV are taken from the THE HOLY BIBLE, ENGLISH STANDARD VERSION (ESV): Scriptures taken from THE HOLY BIBLE, ENGLISH STANDARD VERSION ® Copyright© 2001 by Crossway, a publishing ministry of Good News Publishers. Used by permission.

Printed in the United States of America

CONTENTS

Introduction v

Chapter 1: Those Adults Who… 1
Chapter 2: Those Who Actively Assemble to
           Worship God 21
Chapter 3: Those Who Think On… 41
Chapter 4: Those Who Put On… 61
Chapter 5: Those Who Actively Demonstrate
           Fruits of the Spirit 85
Chapter 6: Those Who… 119

Concluding Thoughts 127
Appendix 1 131

INTRODUCTION

War, murder, child abuse, trafficking of women and children, riots, terrorism, nationalism, starvation, greed, religious extremism, ego-power, rudeness, poverty, political and personal posturing, power-over, protests, homelessness, disease, earthquakes, global warming, drought, radical patriotism—since the fall of humans in the garden of Eden, these problems have existed.

Those who use the label "Christian" as their reason for taking action to fight for or against this list, always claim to be on the side of God. "If God is with us, who can be against us?" Somehow, throughout history, there have been opposing forces allegedly praying to and expecting answers from the same God. What's going on?

Individuals looking for hope, looking for answers, looking for the reasons these problems still exist in "Christian" nations may ask, "Who and where, are the real Christians, and why aren't they fixing things?" Are they in those cookie-cutter buildings with steeples, large parking lots, and digital billboard signs? Are they the ones with hundreds to thousands of people attending there on Sunday morning? Are they the ones who beg for money on television? Are there rich and poor Christians? If there are real Christians, why are their congregations still segregated by ethnicity? Who is really following what the New Testament commands?

In the United States, there are Republican Christians, Democrat Christians, Independent Christians, military Christians, Christian militias, civilian Christians, red and yellow, Black and White Christians, all claiming God belongs to them and is on their side.[1] What are the qualities, actions, and characteristics of real Christians? If there are so many of them, why aren't they fixing all the problems listed in the opening paragraph? When will we have peace in the world? If there are any real Christians, what do they do? How can I know?

A general search of the Internet for "number of Christian denominations in the world" obviously results in a wide variety of numbers, ranging from around three thousand to over fifty thousand. The true answer is no one really knows. The purpose of this book is not to state one denomination is accurate according to the examples of early Christian congregations presented in the New Testament while another is not. Through the simple use of Scripture, the plan is to provide a clear, Bible-based answer to the question, "Who and where are the real Christians?"

Throughout this book, italics will be used to point out critical words and phrases. Selections of Scripture and definitions will be indented so the reader can add their own notes. In addition, many "human" definitions will be taken from the 1930 edition of the *New Revised Webster Dictionary Self-Pronouncing* for the reason it was not "sanitized" of reli-

---

[1] There are no "red, yellow, black, or white" people. Humans are all different shades of brown. The author prefers the phrase "different shades of right."

gious and spiritual terms. Current dictionaries are found to be sanitized and politically correct, which adulterates the older, more original meaning of many words.

The Christian world is made up of an unbelievable number of distinct groups typically labeled "denominations."

Webster defines a denomination as "a religious organization whose congregations are united in their adherence to its beliefs and practices."[2]

In *Webster* 1930, it is defined as "the act of designating; a sect, class, or division."

Each denomination has its own way of worship, its favorite translation of the Bible, its own songbooks, its own variety of building designs, decorations, accoutrements, accessories, and paraphernalia. There are preachers, ministers, pastors, shepherds, priests, bishops, cardinals, popes, clerics, vicars, parsons, reverends, and monks. There are churches, cathedrals, temples, shrines, and sanctuaries. Who and where are the real Christians?

In the United States, there are terms like Christian college/university, Christian television or radio station, Christian day care, Christian church, Christian bookstore, Christian music, or any number of other Christian-titled businesses, organizations, and groups. A search of the yellow pages will show many differently titled churches.

A search of the New Testament for a name of the assemblies or congregations of Christians results in the passages shown below the definition of "way." Notice the fourth definition.

---

[2] Inc Merriam-Webster, *Merriam-Webster's Collegiate Dictionary*, includes index., eleventh ed. (Springfield, MA.: *Merriam-Webster*, Inc. 2003).

Way in Greek is *hodos*: (1) road, path, way, route; (2) journey, implying a greater distance; (3) way of life, figurative extension of above entries; (4) Christian way of life.

What verses mention this way, this true Christian way of life?

> But Saul, still breathing threats and murder against the disciples of the Lord, went to the high priest and asked him for letters to the synagogues at Damascus, so that if he found any belonging to the Way, men or women, he might bring them bound to Jerusalem. (Acts 9:1–2)

> And when Paul had laid his hands on them, the Holy Spirit came on them, and they began speaking in tongues[3] and prophesying[4]. There were about twelve men in all. And he entered the synagogue and for three months spoke boldly, reasoning and persuading them about the kingdom of God. But when some became stubborn and continued in unbelief, speaking evil of the Way before the congregation, he withdrew from them and took the disciples with him, reasoning daily in the hall of Tyrannus. This continued for two years, so that all the residents

---

[3] Recognized, different languages, not nonsensical babbling
[4] Preaching and teaching, not telling the future

of Asia heard the word of the Lord, both Jews and Greeks. (Acts 19:6–10)

Now after these events Paul resolved in the Spirit to pass through Macedonia and Achaia and go to Jerusalem, saying, "After I have been there, I must also see Rome." And having sent into Macedonia two of his helpers, Timothy and Erastus, he himself stayed in Asia for a while. 23 About that time there arose no little disturbance concerning the Way. (Acts 19:21–23)

But this I confess to you, that according to the Way, which they call a sect, I worship the God of our fathers, believing everything laid down by the Law and written in the Prophets, having a hope in God, which these men themselves accept, that there will be a resurrection of both the just and the unjust. (Acts 24:14–15)

But Felix, having a rather accurate knowledge of the Way, put them off, saying, "When Lysias the tribune comes down, I will decide your case." Then he gave orders to the centurion that he should be kept in custody but have some liberty, and that none of his friends should be prevented from attending to his needs. (Acts 24:22–23)

The label *Christian* was first used as referenced in Acts 11:26b: "And in Antioch the disciples (followers of Jesus) were first called Christians." As far as an inclusive name for Christians who gathered together to worship God, "the Way" is the only term found in the New Testament. Typically, around the world today, the name of a particular denomination is followed by, or prefaced by, the word *church*. Almost all English New Testament translations used the word *church* incorrectly. Throughout the rest of this book, the terms *the Way* and *congregation/assembly* will be used as opposed to *church*. The reason for using these words is based on the most accurate definition of the word church.

Church may not be what you think!

Church: noun. 1. a building for public and especially Christian worship.[5]

The 1930 edition of the *New Revised Webster Dictionary Self-Pronouncing* lists as its first definition for church, "a building set apart or consecrated for divine worship."

The Greek word for consecrate is *hagiazō*: (1) dedicate, to service and loyalty to God; (2) make holy, sanctify, to cause one to have the quality of holiness; (3) honor as holy, hallow, feel reverence, regard as holy, and cannot be applied to any physical object.

---

[5] Inc Merriam-Webster, *Merriam-Webster's Collegiate Dictionary.*, Includes index., Eleventh ed. (Springfield, Mass.: Merriam-Webster, Inc., 2003).

The New Testament verses mentioned in the definition apply only to Christians. A true Christian can be made holy but not buildings, land, or monuments.

Is a church people or a building?

> The word 'church' is of dubious origins. From where is it derived? It cannot be from the Greek ecclesia, normally translated church, because there is no etymological link, either from Latin or Greek. Walafrid Strabo who lived 808–849 [A.D.] was a Frankish Monk and Theological Writer who came up with a solution; and this has stayed with us since. His guess was that 'church' came from the Greek for 'Lord's House.' There is, however, no mention of a structural building in the early history of Christianity. Bible translations commonly use the word 'church' to denote a body of Christians who, in the New Testament, met in houses.[6]

In Keith Sisman's thoroughly researched book, *The Devil's Door*, he clearly documented that until the 1600s Christians met in homes for their worship activities. The use of buildings was started by the Catholics who took former pagan temple structures and converted them into their "churches." The Greek word commonly and incorrectly,

---

[6] The Devil's Door - The Cult of the Dead by Keith Sisman ©2017 Forbidden Books, United Kingdom, pg. 604.

translated as "church" is *ekklesia* noun. feminine.; congregation, an individual assembly of Christians, usually with leaders who conform to a standard, and have worship practices, with members interacting, more or less local.

Real Christians from during the time of the New Testament until the mid-1600s met in family homes, not giant buildings costing hundreds of thousands or even millions of dollars! These congregations were local and independent of others.

There was no national headquarters. There were no human originated bylaws or codes of conduct. There were no presidents or boards of directors. In the search for where and who are the real Christians, it begins with people, not buildings.

Can real Christians be found in a giant building with hundreds or thousands of members? Possibly. But they are frequently concerned by the lack of a sense of community, the presence of cliques, or factions and decorations, activities, and celebrations that are not in line with the simplicity of the model presented in the New Testament. In addition, with the global influence of the coronavirus pandemic starting in 2020, almost all congregations meeting in church buildings aren't! If most real Christians are not found in the various denominational structures, where are they likely to be found?

The New Testament describes several occasions where the first Christians met in private homes for their worship activities.

> When the day of Pentecost arrived, they were all together in one place. And suddenly there came from heaven a sound like a mighty rushing wind, and it filled the entire house where they were sitting. (Acts 2:1–2)

> Greet Prisca and Aquila, my fellow workers in Christ Jesus, who risked their necks for my life, to whom not only I give thanks but all the assembled Christians of the Gentiles give thanks as well. Greet also the assembled Christians in their house. Greet my beloved Epaenetus, who was the first convert to Christ in Asia. (Romans 16:3–5)

> The assembled Christians of Asia send you greetings. Aquila and Prisca, together with the assembled Christians in their house, send you hearty greetings in the Lord. (1 Corinthians 16:19)

> Give my greetings to the brothers at Laodicea, and to Nympha and the assem-

bled Christians in her house. (Colossians 4:15)

Paul, a prisoner for Christ Jesus, and Timothy our brother, To Philemon our beloved fellow worker and Apphia our sister and Archippus our fellow soldier, and the assembled Christians in your house. (Philemon 1–2)

He said, "Go into the city to a certain man and say to him, 'The Teacher says, My time is at hand. I will keep the Passover at your house with my disciples.'" (Matthew 26:18)

The word *church* was inserted in New Testament translations around AD 1200 as a replacement and mistranslation of the Greek word *ekklesia*. We can then state the first Christians who met and worshipped together in towns and villages were identified as a congregation or an assembly of the Way, not a church.

Sadly, incorrect traditions and man-generated titles have corrupted the original definition of Christians who gathered together as the feminine noun congregation or assembly. There is a reason why Christians were described by a feminine noun.

The New Testament refers to congregations of Christians as the bride of Christ.

> Husbands, love your wives, as Christ loved the congregations of Christians and gave himself up for her, that he might sanctify her, having cleansed her by the washing of water with the Word, so that he might present the church to himself in splendor, without spot or wrinkle or any such thing, that she might be holy and without blemish. (Ephesians 5:25–27)

Note: Jesus is "the Word." See John 1:1–5.

In those denominations trying to follow the model presented in the New Testament for how Christians are to live their lives, a person who is not a Christian may go through some form of instruction or teaching prior to their being baptized, if they are baptized at all. In some denominations, the congregation's leaders must give their approval for a person to be baptized or sprinkled. The New Testament examples show the decision to become a Christian is solely the responsibility of the individual, not a committee. It is not uncommon for the person, after joining the church, to be congratulated by members of a congregation. After that, "We will be praying for you!" is the statement offered before the new Christian faces the world. Other statements include, "Hope to see you on Sunday and in the Wednesday Bible class!" However, a person wanting to become a Christian does not "join a church." This topic will be covered in depth in chapter 1.

Sadly, many new Christians, and probably some who've been "saved" for a few years, are not aware that the Christian life is a journey filled with learning, study, prayer, times of joy and times of sadness. The Christian life does not end with becoming a Christian. For real Christians, while life in the physical body ends at death, the spiritual element, the soul, continues eternally, either in heaven or in hell. More on this later. For now, please keep this quote from C. S. Lewis in mind: "You don't have a soul. You are a soul. You have a body."

This book provides an easy-to-understand model of the Christian life as defined by the simplicity of many verses from the New Testament. At the end of each chapter will be questions for small groups of Christians to discuss as their journey toward spiritual growth, wisdom, and maturity progresses. Throughout the book, Greek definitions of key words are used to clarify the original intent, and substance of, the inspired writers.

The following six-part model shows there is more to being a real Christian than simply claiming to be one. Part 1 of the model is the only piece that is done in sequence. Parts 2 through 6 are done in sequence, but the various areas under each major category can be worked on individually or collectively.

Depending on the individual, there can be overlap among some items, and that is to be expected as one matures spiritually.

1. Those adults who…
   - hear the Word of God
   - believe the Word of God
   - repent of the former life of sin
   - confess that Jesus is the Son of God
   - be fully immersed in water (baptism) for the forgiveness of sin

2. Those adult Christians who actively assemble to worship God by…
   - singing together
   - taking part in Communion
   - praying together
   - studying in groups of two or more

3. Those adult Christians who think on…
   - whatever is true
   - whatever is honorable
   - whatever is just
   - whatever is pure
   - whatever is lovely
   - whatever is commendable
   - whatever is excellent
   - anything worthy of praise

4. Those adult Christians who put on…
   - a compassionate heart
   - kindness
   - humility
   - meekness

- patience
- bearing with one another
- forgiveness
- love

5. Those adult Christians who actively demonstrate the fruits of the Spirit
   - love
   - joy
   - peace
   - patience
   - kindness
   - goodness
   - faithfulness
   - gentleness
   - self-control

6. Adult Christians who…
   - set aside money, food, clothing, etc. as a part of a weekly, planned budget so the fruits of the Spirit can be actively demonstrated. This is not part of the first day of the week—Sunday *worship* activities.

Given that so many denominations have their own way of practicing their human-invented customs and traditions, and given that so many do not seem to follow the simple plan of the New Testament, where and who are the real Christians?

One important caution is found in the following passage:

> Do not be unequally yoked with unbelievers. For what partnership has righteousness with lawlessness? Or what fellowship has light with darkness? What accord has Christ with Belial?[7] Or what portion does a believer share with an unbeliever? What agreement has the temple of God with idols? For we are the temple of the living God; as God said, "I will make my dwelling among them and walk among them, and I will be their God, and they shall be my people. Therefore go out from their midst, and be separate from them, says the Lord, and touch no unclean thing; then I will welcome you, and I will be a father to you, and you shall be sons and daughters to me, says the Lord Almighty." (2 Corinthians 6:14–18)

The Greek word for unequally yoked is *heterozugeo*: (1) to come under an unequal or different yoke, to be unequally yoked; (1.a.) to have fellowship with one who is not an equal.

The Greek word for unbeliever is *apistos*: (1) unfaithful, faithless, (not to be trusted, perfidious [disloyal]); (2)

---

[7] a pagan god or title

incredible; (2.a.) of things; (3) unbelieving, incredulous; (3.a.) without trust (in God).

The argument I will use is, if one can wear an army uniform with medals, ribbons, patches, and the rank insignia of a captain, and if that person has never been in the army, is that person a deceptive fraud and a fake? If so-called Christians add or take away from the basic model found in the New Testament for each area of this book, then can one say they truly believe the written Word of God? Caution must be exercised when those who call themselves Christians but never do what is both commanded and expected try to get others to worship with them. By not accepting and following the commands of Jesus, are they not unbelievers?

Unbelievers, frauds, and fakes have a habit of adding to or taking away from God's Word to make it better fit the current political, social, military, sports, or economic situation. Both the Old and New Testament have references to adding or taking away from God's Word.

> You shall not add to the word that I command you, nor take from it, that you may keep the commandments of the Lord your God that I command you. (Deuteronomy 4:2)

> Everything that I command you, you shall be careful to do. You shall not add to it or take from it. (Deuteronomy 12:32)

> Do not add to his words, lest he rebuke you and you be found a liar. (Proverbs 30:6)

> I warn everyone who hears the words of the prophecy of this book: if anyone adds to them, God will add to him the plagues described in this book, and if anyone takes away from the words of the book of this prophecy, God will take away his share in the tree of life and in the holy city, which are described in this book. (Revelation 22:18–19)

We close the introduction with this encouraging passage:

> Come to me, all who labor and are heavy laden, and I will give you rest. Take my yoke upon you, and learn from me, for I am gentle and lowly in heart, and you will find rest for your souls. For my yoke is easy, and my burden is light. (Matthew 11:28–30)

Introduction questions and challenges

1. Go back and read the opening paragraph of this chapter. In your personal life history, can you

identify any instances when Christians fixed any of those problems?
2. From your point of view, list those characteristics you feel define a real Christian. What New Testament verses support your view on those characteristics?
3. Discuss the characteristics you feel define who you are right now.

CHAPTER 1

Those Adults Who...

> You can become a Christian by going to church about as easily as you can become a car by sleeping in your garage.
>
> —Garrison Keillor

People faced with making life-altering decisions are often driven by a single emotion as the foundation for that decision. Most emotions can be placed into two main categories: positive or negative. Synonyms include helpful or harmful, service oriented or self-oriented, sharing or selfish, love based or hate based, enthusiastic or apathetic. The list could continue, but it is easy to identify the driving emotion behind a decision that is either beneficial or detrimental to one's life. Adults who are real Christians use patient, logical thought processes combined with physical, emotional, and spiritual actions. The following topics and the Scripture support those thoughts and actions.

1. *Hear the Word of God.*

> So faith comes from hearing, and hearing through the word of Christ. (Romans 10:17)

> Let me ask you only this: Did you receive the Spirit by works of the law or by hearing with faith? (Galatians 3:2)

Suppose a loving, caring parent tells a child to clean his room; how does the child know what to do? The parent tells him and then shows him what to do. The parent may share in the cleaning activities until the child understands what the parent expects. The same method applies to adults who are interested in their spiritual salvation. The passage from Romans is easy to understand and quite clear on what is required to begin the process of individual spiritual development. One's faith in God, Jesus, and the Holy Spirit first happens when one hears teaching by a Christian, using the word of Christ, the New Testament, as the study resource. It is important to accept no other resource is either necessary or required. While study guides can be helpful, such as a Bible dictionary to clarify individual names recorded in the Bible and geographically locating towns, rivers, of regions, they are only supportive tools. The real Christian knows and comprehends the word *do*.

> But be doers of the word, and not hearers only, deceiving yourselves. (James 1:22)

Real Christians "do" as opposed to sitting and doing nothing. Some denominational members claim the Holy Spirit somehow entered their body and told them to do this or that action in order for them to be saved. The passage from Galatians is also clear on how one receives faith. One cannot claim a simple physical action or compliance with a human or Old Testament law gave them faith. If faith comes by hearing, then to enter into the process of becoming a real Christian, the individual must believe something they heard. Just as a father telling a child to jump into his arms, without going through the action, the child will not learn to believe she will be safely caught in her father's arms. The child heard the command and now must do something to believe it will be safe to follow the command.

The Greek word for hear is *akouō*: (1) hear; (2) be able to hear, as opposed to being deaf; (3) receive news, normally by word of mouth; (4) pay attention to, to believe and respond; (5) obey, listen and conform to what was heard; (6) understand, comprehend.

Notice the fourth and fifth definitions. Clearly, there is more to hearing the Word of God than idly sitting in a worship service or Bible class without being actively involved by paying attention, believing and responding, and obeying what was heard.

The Greek word for believe is *pisteuō*: (1) think to be true, to believe, implying trust; (2) trust, faith, believe to the extent of complete trust; (3) have Christian faith, become a believer the Gospel; (4) entrust, put something into the care of another.

The one wanting to become a real Christian must think about what has been discovered in the Word of God, trust and begin developing a faith in the truth of the Word, and recognize real Christians have put their lives in the hands of a loving God.

2. *Believe the Word of God.*

> For God so *loved* the world, that he gave his only Son, that whoever believes in him should not perish but have eternal life. For God did not send his Son into the world to condemn the world, but in order that the world might be saved through him. Whoever believes in him is not condemned, but whoever does not believe is condemned already, because he has not believed in the name of the only Son of God. (John 3:16–18)

> He said to them, "You are from below; I am from above. You are of this world; I am not of this world. I told you

that you would die in your sins, for unless you believe that I am he you will die in your sins." (John 8:23–24)

Now Jesus did many other signs in the presence of the disciples, which are not written in this book; but these are written so that you may believe that Jesus is the Christ, the Son of God, and that by believing you may have life in his name. (John 20:30–31)

The key word in this passage from John is found in verse 16: loved. God is asking the potential real Christian to believe that Jesus is His Son. How does a child believe what the parent says? By the parent using everything available to show and teach the child what needs to be done to complete the task. How does God allow one to believe what He says? By providing a detailed account of the life of Jesus and additional information about the history of early Christians, combined with letters written by the God-inspired apostles of Jesus, giving further guidance on how to worship God and how to live the real Christian life.

If a child makes a mistake, a good parent will recognize the child simply is being a child, not a little adult. A good parent will gently talk to the child about the mistake and encourage the child to try again. In a sense, the parent is helping the child realize why the mistake was made and how to correct it. The saying, "If you always do what you've always done, you will always get what you always got" comes to mind. If one has heard and understood the Word of God and truly believes in that Word, then that person can easily grasp what actions in the past were pulling them away from God and His offer of salvation. They can then make the correct decision to commit to never making those mistakes again. The Bible describes this as repenting or turning away from past actions.

3. *Repent of the former life of sin.*

Real Christians, in the process of changing their lives, must physically, emotionally, and spiritually do things differently than before they came in contact with the Word of God. Some may seem to change their behavior, but without a change in attitude and thought, the change will be superficial and temporary.

The Greek word for repent is *metanoeō*: repent, to change one's life, based on complete change of attitude and thought concerning sin and righteousness.

> Repent therefore, and turn again, that your sins may be blotted out. (Acts 3:19)

> The times of ignorance God overlooked, but now he commands all people everywhere to repent, because he has fixed a day on which he will judge the world in righteousness by a man whom he has appointed; and of this he has given assur-

ance to all by raising him from the dead. (Acts 17:30–31)

Some denominations use these verses by themselves—and out of context—to claim, if one believes and repents, that's all that needs to be done to be saved. Later we will discuss what it means to have sins blotted out or removed. Turning away from a previous life of sinful, unhealthy, damaging behaviors may mean the loss of friends, a change in jobs, and ridicule by others who do not understand repentance.

Some may feel a sense of defeat and failure by leaving behind what they once thought was the good life. Many live under the false promise of freedom provided by a government without realizing the freedoms real Christians enjoy have very little to do with the physical world. More on this later.

Once a person has heard the Word of God, believed it, and made the decision to turn away from the past, a verbal statement must be made confessing that Jesus is who He claimed to be in the New Testament.

The Greek word for confess is *homologeō*: (1) profess, to confess allegiance; (2) admit, confess, acknowledge bad behavior; (3) declare, make an emphatic assertion.

A synonym for confess is acknowledge.

4. *Confess that Jesus is the Son of God.*

Anyone who has served on a jury is familiar with the question often asked by prosecuting attorneys: "Do you confess to the crime?" The attorney is looking for the defendant to publicly answer either "yes" or "no."

> So everyone who acknowledges me before men, I also will acknowledge before my Father who is in heaven, but whoever denies me before men, I also will deny before my Father who is in heaven. (Matthew 10:32–33)

> Because, if you confess with your mouth that Jesus is Lord and believe in your heart that God raised him from the dead, you will be saved. (Romans 10:9)

In the case of one wanting to become a real Christian, the confession is a two-part action. First, the person admits or confesses sins committed in the past and, second, publicly states they believe or acknowledge Jesus as the one true Son of God. Again, certain denominations will use Romans 10:9 alone and out of context to prove if one simply confesses and "accepts Jesus as their Savior," they will be saved. Their error is not looking at all the verses Jesus spoke about the process of salvation.

5. *Be fully immersed in water (baptism) for the forgiveness of sins.*

Another necessary action to be done by one wanting to be a real Christian is being baptized, after expressing sincere repentance of previous sins. The Greek word for baptize is *baptizomai*: wash, assumedly by dipping, in a ceremonial way, baptize, to ceremonially cleanse, with the visible agent of water, to show purity and initiation into Christ through repentance.

> And he said to them, "Go into all the world and proclaim the gospel to the whole creation. Whoever believes and is baptized will be saved, but whoever does not believe will be condemned. (Mark 16:15–16)

> And Jesus came and said to them, "All authority in heaven and on earth has been given to me. Go therefore and make disciples of all nations, baptizing them in the name of the Father and of the Son and of the Holy Spirit, teaching them to observe all that I have commanded you. And behold, I am with you always, to the end of the age." (Matthew 28:18–20)

Jesus commands those being baptized to be baptized "in the name of the Father, of the Son, and of the Holy Spirit." The command is simple, and any denomination that adds to or takes away from this simple command invalidates the baptism.

> Let all the house of Israel therefore know for certain that God has made him both Lord and Christ, this Jesus whom you crucified." Now when they heard this they were cut to the heart, and said to Peter and the rest of the apostles, "Brothers, what shall we do?" And Peter said to them, "Repent and be baptized every one of you in the name of Jesus Christ for the forgiveness of your sins, and you will receive the gift of the Holy Spirit. For the promise is for you and for your children and for all who are far off, everyone whom the Lord our God calls to himself." And with many other words he bore witness and continued to exhort them, saying, "Save yourselves from this crooked generation." So those who received his word were baptized, and there were added that day about three thousand souls. (Acts 2:36–41)

This passage clearly states the reason one must be baptized: to have sins forgiven. In addition, the one being baptized, after hearing the Word of God being taught, repenting of past sins, confessing that sins were committed and that Jesus is the Son of God, now receives the gift of the Holy Spirit.

There is much confusion in the denominational world about this phrase. The New Testament eliminates this confusion. Any person who has not been baptized does not have the Holy Spirit living in them. The Holy Spirit has a purpose, and we will discuss that in chapter 5.

If a mother says to her child, "When you clean your room, I will give you the gift of a cookie," the child easily understands the simplicity of the statement made by the mother. "Do this, and I will do…" The same logic applies here: "Do this, be baptized, and I (God through Jesus) will give you the Holy Spirit." Some claim this now permits new Christians to do miracles, speak in unintelligible words ("tongues"), and other seemingly impossible actions. This is not the case. Miracles ceased with the completion of the writing of the New Testament.

> Love never ends. As for prophecies, they will pass away; as for tongues, they will cease; as for knowledge, it will pass away. For we know in part and we prophesy in part, but when the perfect comes, the partial will pass away. (1 Corinthians 13:8–10)

These verses tell us "knowledge," a reference to Old Testament prophecies about the coming of Jesus, have "passed away." Why? Because the New Testament, the new covenant, tells us Jesus, the Messiah, did come! The miraculous speaking in different, known languages done by the Apostles has ceased.

Knowledge, a reference to knowing the old covenant/law, has ended with the arrival of Jesus and the finished writing of the New Testament. The new covenant provided by the life of Jesus on earth is complete. It is the perfect, absolute final writing for Christians.

> Then Philip opened his mouth, and beginning with this Scripture he told him the good news about Jesus. And as they were going along the road they came to some water, and the eunuch said, "See, here is water! What prevents me from being baptized?" And he commanded the chariot to stop, and they both went down into the water, Philip and the eunuch, and he baptized him. And when they came up out of the water, the Spirit of the Lord carried Philip away, and the eunuch saw him no more, and went on his way rejoicing. (Acts 8:35–36, 38–39)

Note: The most accurate translations do not include verse 37.

> And Philip said, "If you believe with all your heart, you may." And he replied, "I believe that Jesus Christ is the Son of God."

Some denominations believe sprinkling a few drops of water on one's head is baptism. If that is true, why did the eunuch from Ethiopia go with Philip down into the water instead of standing on the shore and having Philip dribble some water on his head? It is important to read and understand the details provided.

After Philip baptized the eunuch, they came up out of the water, something that would not have happened if Philip only scooped a handful of water to sprinkle on his head. In addition, the eunuch was likely a wealthy man, given he had a chariot with a driver. Earlier in this passage, we are told he was sitting in his chariot, reading from the book of Isaiah. As a court official of Candace, queen of the Ethiopians, who was in charge of all her treasure, it is likely he had containers of food and water for his journey to Jerusalem. Since he had water with him, why did they stop and go down into the water? Because baptism, in addition to getting very wet, is a symbolic act with a spiritual purpose.

> Do you not know that all of us who have been baptized into Christ Jesus were baptized into his death? [4] We were buried therefore with him by baptism into death, in order that, just as Christ was raised from the dead by the glory of the Father, we too might walk in newness of life. (Romans 6:3–4)

Just as Jesus was physically crucified, murdered, buried, then came back alive after his resurrection, one wanting to become a real Christian mirrors that act by being "buried" in water then coming up out of the water, symbolically being resurrected, subsequently walking this planet in the new life of a saved, sin-free Christian. This does not mean the person can never sin again. But it does mean the new Christian doesn't want to sin. This will be discussed in more detail later.

Remember Acts 2:41: "So those who received his word were baptized, and there were added that day about three thousand souls." In the denominational world, the question, "Where do you go to church?" is frequently asked. Or "What church did you join?" Keep in mind the original definitions of "church" and "assembly" or congregation of Christians. The one being baptized does not join a church. Verse 41 clearly states, after being baptized, their soul is added to the body of Christ.

> For just as the body is one and has many members, and all the members of the body, though many, are one body, so it is with Christ. For in one Spirit we were all baptized into one body—Jews or Greeks, slaves or free—and all were made to drink of one Spirit. (1 Corinthians 12:12–13)

If all real Christians are collectively described as one body, the body of Christ, then there cannot be more than one body. Sadly, there are thousands of denominations and millions of pseudo-Christians claiming to be the body of Christ.

Verse 12 states there are many members of the one body. As C. S. Lewis stated, we have a body. In the New Testament, Jesus had one physical body. Now he has one spiritual body, those who simply call themselves "Christians." They use no denominational titles or labels added by human religious leaders.

Humans have only one body, and every part of the human body has a function. Every Christian has a function. One cannot sever a hand, place it in a chemical solution, and then claim it is a new body. A denomination cannot use only select verses in the Bible while ignoring the rest and claim to be the only real body of Christ. Those that do have walked away from Jesus and are no longer connected to anything having to do with real Christians.

> So then, the law was our guardian until Christ came, in order that we might be justified by faith. But now that faith has come, we are no longer under a guardian, for in Christ Jesus you are all sons of God, through faith. For as many of you as were baptized into Christ have put on Christ. There is neither Jew nor Greek, there is neither slave nor free, there is no male and female, for you are all one in Christ Jesus. And if you are Christ's, then you are Abraham's offspring, heirs according to promise. (Galatians 3:24–29)

Some denominations claim the Ten Commandments as the foundation for their belief system. From time to time, they make the news by protesting the removal of the Ten Commandments from a marble monument outside a county or state courthouse. They clearly have fallen in the trap of narrow-minded traditions that ignore what the Bible really says. A focused study of the Old Testament will result in the student realizing the "Ten Commandments" were the first of over six hundred commands! Why aren't all six hundred plus commands engraved on the courthouse monuments?

Many denominations also try to combine commands from the Old Testament law with the New Testament commands from Jesus. In Galatians 2:24–25, it is clear, Jesus's arrival and the introduction of the concept of faith as an integral part of spiritual change did away with the old laws found in the Old Testament.

> Love bears all things, believes all things, hopes all things, endures all things. Love never ends. As for prophecies, they will pass away; as for tongues, they will cease; as for knowledge, it will pass away. For we know in part and we prophesy in part, but when the perfect comes, the partial will pass away. When I was a child, I spoke like a child, I thought like a child, I reasoned like a child. When I became a man, I gave up childish ways. For now we see in a mirror dimly, but then face to face.

> Now I know in part; then I shall know fully, even as I have been fully known. So now faith, hope, and love abide, these three; but the greatest of these is love. (1 Corinthians 13:7–13)

> Beloved, let us love one another, for love is from God, and whoever loves has been born of God and knows God. Anyone who does not love does not know God, because God is love. (1 John 4:7–8)

These two passages complete the process and bring everything back to God. Beginning in verse 8, we find a list of things that will go away "when the perfect comes." This is a reference to the complete New Testament. We have it. It has come. Therefore, the prophecies found in the Old Testament no longer apply because they have already come true. The miraculous ability of the apostles to speak in different, recognizable languages (tongues) has stopped. Using the old laws to gain knowledge has gone away with the coming of Jesus and the New Testament. Those who used, and still attempt to use, the old laws only know in part and prophesy (preach or teach) in part. The partial is gone! It is done away with! Because of the New Testament, real Christians can know fully the Word of God as it applies to them. One very important verse is 1 John 4:8b: God is love.

Everything He does is based on love. Do we understand everything God does? Of course not.

> For my thoughts are not your thoughts, neither are your ways my ways, declares the Lord. For as the heavens are higher than the earth, so are my ways higher than your ways and my thoughts than your thoughts. (Isaiah 55:8–9)

By our faith in God, we accept we cannot begin to comprehend all He does. And we do not need to understand. We have the knowledge of what one must do to become a real Christian and then teach others, and that is enough. Unfortunately, in many denominations, once an adult joins the church, they are on their own to figure out what to do next. There are thousands of books written by celebrity religious authors on how to live the Christian life. Many are focused on getting more wealth. Many are focused on "Look how important I can be in the world!" as evidenced by their portrait photographs on the cover of their books.

A new Christian has the faith to make a choice to take the next steps in the process of living a Christian life. As mentioned before, the word *do* is now more essential than ever before.

> What good is it, my brothers, if someone says he has faith but does not have works? Can that faith save him? If

a brother or sister is poorly clothed and lacking in daily food, and one of you says to them, "Go in peace, be warmed and filled," without giving them the things needed for the body, what good is that? So also faith by itself, if it does not have works, is dead. But someone will say, "You have faith and I have works." Show me your faith apart from your works, and I will show you my faith by my works. You believe that God is one; you do well. Even the demons believe—and shudder! Do you want to be shown, you foolish person, that faith apart from works is useless? Was not Abraham our father justified by works when he offered up his son Isaac on the altar? You see that faith was active along with his works, and faith was completed by his works; and the Scripture was fulfilled that says, "Abraham believed God, and it was counted to him as righteousness"—and he was called a friend of God. You see that a person is justified by works and not by faith alone. And in the same way was not also Rahab the prostitute justified by works when she received the messengers and sent them out by another way? For as the body apart from the spirit is dead, so also faith apart from works is dead. (James 2:14–26)

If faith without works is dead, the new Christian may ask, "What works are necessary to validate my faith?" The next chapters, using clear and simple-to-understand Scripture, provide the guidelines real Christians will use as they move from coming up out of the water to living their lives on this temporary planet.

Chapter 1 questions and challenges

1. In your daily life at home, work, school, or out in public, why do you do what you do? Where did you learn to do what you do? Who were your teachers? Who influenced you the most in a positive way?
2. If you are a Christian, what do you consider to be the important parts of worshipping God? Where did you learn these? Have you ever felt like leaving where you worship and going someplace else? Why or why not?

Chapter 2

Those Who Actively Assemble to Worship God

Worship changes the worshiper into the image of the One worshiped.

—Jack Hayford

In many denominations, the assembly of their members is focused on entertaining the masses. There are elevated stages, professional lighting and sound systems, strobe lights, live bands, paid professional singers, choruses, soloists, and preachers, pastors, reverends, elders, bishops, cardinals, popes, etc. who try to do everything they can to maintain the interest of the crowd. To an outsider, the appearance is similar to a Broadway musical show or a rock concert.

The Greek word for worship is *proskyneō*: (1) worship, bow as an act of allegiance or regard; (2) prostrate oneself before, kneel down before as an act of reverence.

Many surveys of those leaving one denomination for another list the primary reason for leaving as boredom. "I don't get anything out of the program." Once again, man-made traditions and ignorance of New Testament examples have pulled so many away from the basic model of true worship. Real Christians accept and willingly understand that worship activities must be focused on God. There is no example of being entertained by a lectern-pounding, Bible-slamming, running-across-the-stage preacher. When we look at how Jesus presented His messages, commands, and instructions, the New Testament has the following references about Jesus sitting down.

- Matthew 5:1; 13:2; 13:48; 15:29
- Mark 9:35; 12:41; 16:19
- Luke 4:20; 5:3
- John 6:13; 8:3
- Hebrews 1:3

Looking at the denominational world, it is quite rare to see a preacher in a Sunday morning service sitting down to quietly and gently share the message, conversing with the people. Typically, there is an elevated stage, putting the preacher above his congregation, combined with a massive wooden lectern surrounded by planters filled with artificial flowers, padded comfortable chairs for the elders, a heated baptistery, microphones, projectors and automatic screens, and of course, the inevitable PowerPoint presentation. It is also common to have a "numbers" board hanging at the front of the auditorium. On the board will be last Sunday's attendance, both a.m. and p.m., Wednesday's Bible class attendance, the budgeted and hoped-for dollar amount of the contribution, and last Sunday's dollar amount actually contributed. There may also be a second board with a list of page numbers in the hymnal for the songs that will be sung during the service. One other item of interest is the clock. One will usually be mounted on the wall in the back of the auditorium so the preacher can make sure to not go over the allotted time. Heaven forbid if the sermon goes over the scheduled twenty to thirty minutes shown in the printed worship program handout!

Interestingly enough, there are no commands anywhere in the New Testament for these items. None! With these thoughts in mind, reflect on the feeling and attitude of the listeners in this verse:

> On the first day of the week, when we were gathered together to break bread, Paul talked with them, intending to depart on the next day, and he prolonged his speech until midnight. There were many lamps in the upper room where we were gathered. And a young man named Eutychus, sitting at the window, sank into a deep sleep as Paul talked still longer. And being overcome by sleep, he fell down from the third story and was taken up dead. But

> Paul went down and bent over him, and taking him in his arms, said, "Do not be alarmed, for his life is in him." And when Paul had gone up and had broken bread and eaten, he conversed with them a long while, until daybreak, and so departed. And they took the youth away alive, and were not a little comforted. (Acts 20:7–12)

There are several key items to notice in this passage. Those Christians met on the first day of the week, Sunday, to first break bread. This is a reference to the Communion, discussed in the next bullet point. Next, Paul talked *with* them as opposed to talking *to* them from an elevated power-over position. Can you imagine listening and conversing with a preacher beginning in the daylight and going until the next morning! There was no multimillion-dollar building. They met in the upper room of a home. How simple and personal was this early worship gathering!

In other passages, we learn one key purpose for gathering together was to celebrate the life of Jesus through eating of unleavened bread and drinking wine, which together symbolically represent the body and blood of Jesus. In the denominational world, the Communion part of the worship service is treated as something that must be completed as quickly as possible, again, so the congregation doesn't get impatient by looking at the time. Still others only provide for Communion to be done monthly or only on Easter and Christmas. There are increasing numbers of denominations offering traditional worship on Sunday and modern worship with Communion on Saturday night, targeting the younger audiences.

In other parts of the world, outside the United States, there are small groups of Christians who meet in small rented spaces, and more time is spent in the Communion part of worship than much of the other parts that will be covered below. The command Jesus gave the early Christians was simple. Read on!

- *Take part in Communion*

> Now as they were eating, Jesus took bread, and after blessing it broke it and gave it to the disciples, and said, "Take, eat; this is my body." And he took a cup, and when he had given thanks he gave it to them, saying, "Drink of it, all of you, for this is my blood of the covenant, which is poured out for many for the forgiveness of sins. I tell you I will not drink again of this fruit of the vine until that day when I drink it new with you in my Father's kingdom." (Matthew 26:26–29)

> And as they were eating, he took bread, and after blessing it broke it and gave it to them, and said, "Take; this is my body." And he took a cup, and when he had given thanks he gave it to them, and they all drank of it. And he said to them,

"This is my blood of the covenant, which is poured out for many. Truly, I say to you, I will not drink again of the fruit of the vine until that day when I drink it new in the kingdom of God." (Mark 14:22–25)

And when the hour came, he reclined at table, and the apostles with him. And he said to them, "I have earnestly desired to eat this Passover with you before I suffer. For I tell you I will not eat it until it is fulfilled in the kingdom of God." And he took a cup, and when he had given thanks he said, "Take this, and divide it among yourselves. For I tell you that from now on I will not drink of the fruit of the vine until the kingdom of God comes." And he took bread, and when he had given thanks, he broke it and gave it to them, saying, "This is my body, which is given for you. Do this in remembrance of me." And likewise the cup after they had eaten, saying, "This cup that is poured out for you is the new covenant in my blood. (Luke 22:14–20)

The cup of blessing that we bless, is it not a participation in the blood of Christ? The bread that we break, is it not a participation in the body of Christ? Because there is one bread, we who are many are one body, for we all partake of the one bread. Consider the people of Israel: are not those who eat the sacrifices participants in the altar? What do I imply then? That food offered to idols is anything, or that an idol is anything? No, I imply that what pagans sacrifice they offer to demons and not to God. I do not want you to be participants with demons. You cannot drink the cup of the Lord and the cup of demons. You cannot partake of the table of the Lord and the table of demons. (1 Corinthians 10:16–21)

For I received from the Lord what I also delivered to you, that the Lord Jesus on the night when he was betrayed took bread, and when he had given thanks, he broke it, and said, "This is my body which is for you. Do this in remembrance of me." In the same way also he took the cup, after supper, saying, "This cup is the new covenant in my blood. Do this, as often as you drink it, in remembrance of me." For as often as you eat this bread and drink the cup, you proclaim the Lord's death until he comes. Whoever, therefore, eats the bread or drinks the cup of the Lord in an unworthy manner will be guilty concern-

> ing the body and blood of the Lord. Let a person examine himself, then, and so eat of the bread and drink of the cup. For anyone who eats and drinks without discerning the body eats and drinks judgment on himself. (1 Corinthians 11:23–29)

In the denominational world, one or more of these verses are read to help prepare the minds of those who will eat and drink the bread and wine. The command is for each individual Christian to both eat and drink for a specific purpose: to remember the life of Jesus. Sadly, oftentimes the emphasis is only on the death of Jesus. As a result, when songs are sung as part of the preparation, they are sad, sung very slowly, and everyone tries their best to put on the sad face, usually looking down at the floor, their feet, a Bible, or their phone.

Think about this alternative: Be happy and thankful for the amazing physical life of Jesus! Be happy He did so many miracles. Be happy He demonstrated pure love and compassion. Be happy He was, and is, the only perfect example we have of complete humility before God and man, dying so that salvation would be made available for all of humanity. And most importantly, be happy He was resurrected, spent forty additional days doing even more miracles, and even now is sitting!

> So then the Lord Jesus, after he had spoken to them, was taken up into heaven

and sat down at the right hand of God. (Mark 16:19)

- *Singing*

> I will sing praise with my spirit, but I will sing with my mind also. (1 Corinthians 14:15b)

There are many Christian songbooks in bookstores. Numbering in the hundreds of pages, most are divided into sections or topics. In *Praise for the LORD*,[8] the following is listed in the contents:

> Core Collection . . . 1–800
> Special Collection . . . 801–900
> National Hymns
> Folk Hymns
> Children's Hymns
> Devotional Songs & Hymns
> Expanded Collection . . . 901–990
> Indexes
> Authors
> Tunes, metrical
> Tunes, alphabetical
> Scriptures
> Topics
> First Lines & Titles

---

[8] John P. Wiegland, editor, Mark M. McInteer, publisher, Praise Press, P.O. Box 40304, Nashville, TN 37204, expanded edition. Copyright ©1992.

Joseph Redman

In another song book, *Songs of Faith and Praise*,[9] the following is listed in the table of contents:

God's Praise and Adoration . . . 1–109
God's Love and Grace . . . 110–141
Savior's Praise and Adoration . . . 142–311
Savior's Sacrifice . . . 312–387
Savior's Leadership . . . 388–417
Holy Spirit . . . 418–429
Word of God . . . 430–450
Christian Assurance . . . 451–535
Christian Life . . . 536–620
Christian Mission . . . 621–660
Consecration and Devotion . . . 661–701
Church – One Another . . . 702–759
Prayer . . . 760–849
Heaven . . . 850-900
Heaven's Call . . . 901–951
Spirituals . . . 952–989
Special Themes . . . 990–1030 (Includes children's medley, creation medley, Jesus's birth medley, patriotic medley)
Guide to Indexes and Explanation . . . preceding (sic) 1030
Index of Scripture Text and Readings . . . 1031
Index of Authors, Composers, Arrangers, and Sources of Hymns . . . 1032
Alphabetical Index of Tunes . . . 1037
Index of Scriptures Appearing with Hymn Titles . . . 1039

---

[9] *Conventional Note Edition*, compiled and edited by Alton H. Howard, Howard Publishing Co., Inc., 3117 North 7th Street, West Monroe, LA 71291-2227, Copyright ©1994.

Metrical Index of Tunes . . . 1042
Index of Medleys . . . 1046
Topical Index . . . 1048
General Index . . . 1060

Finally, let's look at a 1937 songbook titled *Devotional Songs*.[10] In the front of the book is this statement: "DEVOTIONAL SONGS with its ninety singable (sic) songs, new and old, represents a sincere effort to present to churches a small yet compact and practical songbook for use in the worship or revival services at a very economical price. Prices . . . 20 ¢ A COPY. $15.00 A 100 PREPAID." At the end of the book is a simple alphabetical general index with no specific sections or divisions. There are no patriotic songs and no children's songs.

In these songbooks, the format of the lyrics and notes are divided into soprano, alto, tenor, and bass parts with standard musical notations, keys, sharps, and flats. Looking at the few verses in the New Testament about singing, it is clear the denominational world decided to make singing and song books a complex, overly structured, minutely detailed collection, able to be directed by only a few talented song leaders, contradicting the simplicity of the Word of God.

Singing praise to God must be with our own personal spirit, that eternal presence we enjoy now and will even more so in heaven, but also with our hearts and minds. In

---
[10] L. O. Sanderson, editor, *A Splendid Revival Compilation, Printed in Shaped Notes Only*, Gospel Advocate Company, Nashville, Tennessee. Copyright, 1937, by Gospel Advocate.

other words, we must think about the words we are singing as we praise God in song.

The Greek word for praise is *aineo*: (1) to praise, extol, to sing praises in honor to God; (2) to allow, recommend; (3) to promise or vow.

Notice the second definition: to sing praises in honor to God. In the previously mentioned two songbooks with the massive tables of content, the bulk of songs have little to do with praising God and much to do with *"me, me, me!"*

The real Christian must truly think deeply on the words being sung. Are we praising self or God?

> Is anyone among you suffering? Let him pray. Is anyone cheerful? Let him sing praise. (James 5:13)

As mentioned before about sad songs being sung prior to the communion, this verse in James seems to suggest it is okay to be cheerful and sing! If there is suffering, don't sing sad songs, pray instead!

> And do not get drunk with wine, for that is debauchery, but be filled with the Spirit, addressing (speaking to) one another in psalms and hymns and spiritual songs, singing and making melody to the Lord with your heart, giving thanks always and for everything to God the Father in the name of our Lord Jesus

> Christ, submitting to one another out of reverence for Christ. (Ephesians 5:18–21)

Paul, when writing to Christians at Ephesus, clearly points out our singing is directed "to the Lord." We sing to (with) other Christians, from the heart, giving thanks to God.

> Let the word of Christ dwell in you richly, teaching and admonishing one another in all wisdom, singing psalms and hymns and spiritual songs, with thankfulness in your hearts to God. (Colossians 3:16)

Again, the singing of the real Christian is directed to honor God. If the focus is on anything else, it falls closer to being labeled *entertainment* and not true worship.

Another part of acceptable worship is the use of prayer.

● *Praying*

> But I say to you, Love your enemies and pray for those who persecute you, so that you may be sons of your Father who is in heaven. For he makes his sun rise on the evil and on the good, and sends rain on the just and on the unjust. (Matthew 5:44–45)

And when you pray, you must not be like the hypocrites. For they love to stand and pray in the synagogues and at the street corners, that they may be seen by others. Truly, I say to you, they have received their reward. But when you pray, go into your room and shut the door and pray to your Father who is in secret. And your Father who sees in secret will reward you. And when you pray, do not heap up empty phrases as the Gentiles do, for they think that they will be heard for their many words. Do not be like them, for your Father knows what you need before you ask him. (Matthew 6:5–8)

Watch and pray that you may not enter into temptation. The spirit indeed is willing, but the flesh is weak. (Matthew 26:41)

But I say to you who hear, Love your enemies, do good to those who hate you, bless those who curse you, pray for those who abuse you. (Luke 6:27–28)

And he told them a parable to the effect that they ought always to pray and not lose heart. (Luke 18:1)

And he came out and went, as was his custom, to the Mount of Olives, and the disciples followed him. And when he came to the place, he said to them, "Pray that you may not enter into temptation." (Luke 22:39–40)

Repent, therefore, of this wickedness of yours, and pray to the Lord that, if possible, the intent of your heart may be forgiven you. (Acts 8:22)

Likewise the Spirit helps us in our weakness. For we do not know what to pray for as we ought, but the Spirit himself intercedes for us with groanings too deep for words. (Romans 8:26)

See that no one repays anyone evil for evil, but always seek to do good to one another and to everyone. Rejoice always, pray without ceasing, give thanks in all circumstances; for this is the will of God in Christ Jesus for you. (1 Thessalonians 5:15–18)

I desire then that in every place the men should pray, lifting holy hands without anger or quarreling. (1 Timothy 2:8)

> Is anyone among you suffering? Let him pray. Is anyone cheerful? Let him sing praise. (James 5:13)

> Is anyone among you sick?[11] Let him call for the elders of the congregation, and let them pray over him, anointing him with oil in the name of the Lord. And the prayer of faith will save the one who is sick, and the Lord will raise him up. And if he has committed sins, he will be forgiven. (James 5:14–15)

> Therefore, confess your sins to one another and pray for one another, that you may be healed. The prayer of a righteous person has great power as it is working. (James 5:16)

It is common in the denominational world to have the following prayers listed in the Schedule of Worship:

The Opening Prayer

The Prayer Before the Sermon (usually combined with a short scripture reading linked to the sermon title)

A Communion Prayer
A Closing Prayer

---

[11] The term "sick" in this verse refers to being spiritually weak.

There are no verses in the New Testament requiring printed schedules of worship with titled types of prayer. Real Christians know they must pray for enemies, for each other, pray constantly (meaning throughout each day and night), pray in private, pray without attempting to make the prayer longer in the hope others might be impressed with how holy the one praying is, and praying with the faith that God will answer.

There are some who become impatient and doubt their faith when God doesn't answer a prayer either immediately or in the way they wanted. Here's a little reminder about how God answers prayer. Sometimes He says, "Yes." Sometimes He says, "No." Sometimes he says, "Not right now. Be patient." And sometimes He says, "Are you kidding!" Even Jesus had to scold his apostles about their faith:

> And when he got into the boat, his disciples followed him. And behold, there arose a great storm on the sea, so that the boat was being swamped by the waves; but he was asleep. And they went and woke him, saying, "Save us, Lord; we are perishing." And he said to them, "Why are you afraid, O you of little faith?" Then he rose and rebuked the winds and the sea, and there was a great calm. And the men marveled, saying, "What sort of man is this, that even winds and sea obey him?" (Matthew 8:23–27)

Another requirement for real Christians is to gather together on Sunday to worship, honor, glorify, and praise God. The requirement for the number to be present is clear and can be accomplished all over the world.

- *Studying in groups of two or more*

> Again I say to you, if two of you agree on earth about anything they ask, it will be done for them by my Father in heaven. For where two or three are gathered in my name, there am I among them. (Matthew 18:19–20)

> And let us consider how to stir up one another to love and good works, not neglecting to meet together, as is the habit of some, but encouraging one another, and all the more as you see the Day drawing near. (Hebrews 10:24–25)

Only two or more real Christians are necessary for God to be in their presence and for them to be in the presence of God as they worship. Matthew 18:19 mentions two Christians on earth agreeing about what they are asking God through prayer—"on the earth!" Notice the clear absence here and, throughout the New Testament, of any reference to a specific country or nation. Only the earth is mentioned. Again the emphasis is on individual Christians, not nations.

The New Testament is explicit that all worship activities are focused on praising God, as opposed to the attendee being entertained. Real Christians are those who are completely thankful for each blessing provided by God every day and enjoy spending time in the presence of God when gathered with other Christians. Real Christians are not clock watchers. Whether the time together is thirty minutes or five hours, real Christians know the joy of being a child of God.

Chapter 2 questions and challenges

1. If you are a Christian, what parts of worship services where you attend fit the simple model provided in the New Testament? What parts don't?
2. Make a list of the activities that do not fit the model. Where did they originate? Who decided to add them to what the Bible says is true worship?
3. Are those activities focused on entertaining the congregation or acknowledging God?

CHAPTER 3

THOSE WHO THINK ON...

> Beware of what you set your mind on
> for that you will surely become.
>
> —Emerson[12]

As mentioned earlier, in many denominations, once one has been baptized, they are left on their own to figure out what to do next. The verses in Philippians 4 were written to purposely clarify the next steps. Given that real Christians accept they are on a lifelong journey, they know the items in this list are not something one perfects and then moves to the next. Real Christians know they

---

[12] Paul Lee Tan, *Encyclopedia of 7700 Illustrations: A Treasury of Illustrations, Anecdotes, Facts and Quotations for Pastors, Teachers and Christian Workers* (Garland TX: Bible Communications, 1996, c1979).

move toward perfection in each of these areas as they travel through life.

> Finally, brothers, whatever is true, whatever is honorable, whatever is just, whatever is pure, whatever is lovely, whatever is commendable, if there is any excellence, if there is anything worthy of praise, think about these things. What you have learned and received and heard and seen in me—practice these things, and the God of peace will be with you. (Philippians 4:8–9)

The Greek word for think is *logizomai*: (1) reason about, ponder, think about; (2) Keep mental record, bear in mind; (3) hold a view, have an opinion.

Notice the Greek word *logizomai* is the root word for logic! Thinking logically demands action, purpose, practice, determination, and prayer. While at first it may seem too much of a challenge to work toward thinking about so many concepts, the old coaching saying comes to mind: "Don't practice until you get it right. Practice until you can't get it wrong!"

A suggestion: When thinking about each area, do not limit yourself.

Obviously, God, Jesus, the Holy Spirit, and the Word of God comes to mind, but it is okay to expand your thinking to include real Christian examples from which you can observe learnable, transferable skills to apply in your daily life.

- *Think on whatever is true.*

The Greek word for true is *alethes*: (1) true, pertaining to what actually occurs; (2) real, not imaginary; (3) honest, truthful, having integrity.

The 1930 *Webster's Dictionary* defines truth as agreement with reality; eternal principle of right, or law of order; veracity; fidelity; fact; realization; conformity to rule or example; righteousness; the right religion.

Current editions of dictionaries rarely, if ever, include "righteousness" or "the right religion!"

When was the last time you saw or read a news report about someone who always spoke the truth? When was the last time you saw or read a news report about someone who never falsified anything in their work or personal life? When was the last time you read a nonfiction book that did not contain any factual errors or misguided facts? In whom do you place greater trust—one who is truthful or one who is not?

> And we know that the Son of God has come and has given us understanding, so that we may know him who is true; and we are in him who is true, in his Son Jesus Christ. He is the true God and eternal life. (1 John 5:20)

A Greek philosopher named Diogenes (412 BC) made himself most unwelcome in Athens by trudging about barefoot without wearing a proper outer robe. He was best known for carrying a lantern during daylight hours, thrusting the lantern in the face of people, saying, "I am looking for an honest man." He never found the man.[13]

What are the indicators of an honest man? Are they physical?

Throughout the country, there are stories about cashiers who accidentally give too much change and the customer returning the difference. There are stories about a package delivery service or the post office, delivering a package to the wrong address and the unintended recipient taking the package to the correct address instead of opening it and keeping what was inside.

Body language experts state that if a person blinks rapidly when answering a question, they may not be telling the truth. As with any expert opinion, caution is necessary. The person may simply have some dust in their eyes. Avoiding eye contact is often an accepted reason to suspect a person is not telling the truth. The problem with that argument is some cultures do not make eye contact until a friendship has been made with the other person.

A child may claim they did not eat the cookies while crumbs and smeared chocolate are all over their face.

From a physical point of view, if one can regularly and routinely observe another person following through on

---

[13] Paul Lee Tan, *Encyclopedia of 7700 Illustrations: A Treasury of Illustrations, Anecdotes, Facts and Quotations for Pastors, Teachers and Christian Workers* (Garland TX: Bible Communications, 1996, c1979).

every action they say they will do, no matter how challenging or difficult the circumstances, we usually say they are true and honest.

● *Think on whatever is honorable.*

In courtrooms, judges are called *Your Honor*. Some groups of people have been labeled as having honor and being worthy of respect based on their previous deeds or actions. Military veterans, police officers, firefighters, emergency medical personnel, and certain volunteers are some of those groups.

The Greek definition of honor is *semnos*: (1) august (respected; dignified), venerable (honored, esteemed), reverend (holy); (2) to be venerated (much-admired) for character, honorable; (2.a.) of persons; (2.b.) of deeds.

Who makes the nightly news broadcasts more often, those who break the law or those who do not break the law? In the workplace, who is the most obvious worker, the one who always arrives early or on time, works hard all day long, is friendly with everyone, is helpful to others, takes vacation time to spend with family, never gossips, politely asks probing questions when a task is not understood, enjoys conversation during lunch, and is the unofficial go-to person for advice or the one who always has an excuse for being late, who does everything possible to avoid real work, doesn't like anyone but himself, tells others to "figure it out for yourself," has accumulated hundreds of hours of vacation time because he is "too important" to be gone, always talks about others behind their backs, will never ask how an unfamiliar task should be done, rarely eats lunch with anyone else, and is the one everybody tries to avoid?

The real Christian humbly understands the importance of those actions described by the first, and usually unnoticed, worker. The real Christian is not aggressively seeking recognition, respect, admiration, or honors from others but knows her actions that are defined by others as honorable behavior will be recognized by God.

● *Think on whatever is just.*

One statement heard around the world is, "We want justice!" This may come from a court decision many disagree with. It may come from what the public believes is an illegal arrest or police shooting. It frequently comes from the poor who want corrupt leaders arrested and punished for corrupt behaviors.

The model designed by God was for rulers to decree what is just. Conversely, if rulers are wicked, denying Him by refusing to do what is just, they will be swept away, removed from their position of power.

> By me kings reign, and rulers decree what is just; by me princes rule, and nobles, all who govern justly. (Proverbs 8:15–16)

> The violence of the wicked will sweep them away, because they refuse to do what is just. (Proverbs 21:7)

Decrees were and are simply the laws established by the ruler or government body approved to make laws. The Hebrew definition mentions the physical activity of cutting out, perhaps describing cuneiform impressions made in clay tablets, in addition to enacting laws. The Greek definition mentions words we use today—doctrines, ordinances, and instructions for right living.

In Hebrew, decree is *chaqaq*: (1)to cut out, decree, inscribe, set, engrave, portray, govern; (1.a.1.) to cut in; (1.a.2.) to cut in or on, cut upon, engrave, inscribe; (1.a.3.) to trace, mark out; (1.a.4.) to engrave, inscribe (of a law); (1.b.1.) to inscribe, enact, decree; (1.b.2.) one who decrees, lawgiver; (1.c.) something decreed, the law; (1.d.) to be inscribed.

In Greek, decree is *dogma*: (1) doctrine, decree, ordinance; (1.a.) of public decrees; (1.b.) of the Roman senate; (1.c.) of rulers; (2) the rules and requirements of the law of Moses; carrying a suggestion of severity and of threatened judgment; (3) of certain decrees of the apostles relative to right living.

To identify a just person, *Webster* can help. Notice the similarity of *Webster's* definition with the Greek!

1930 *Webster's Dictionary*: Just: conformable to divine or human laws; upright; impartial; faithful; exact; regular; fair

In Greek *dikaios* means (1) righteous, observing divine laws; (1.a.) in a wide sense, upright, righteous, virtuous, keeping the commands of God; (1.a.1.) of those who seem to themselves to be righteous, who pride themselves to be righteous, who pride themselves in their virtues, whether real or imagined; (1.a.2.) innocent, faultless, guiltless; (1.a.3.) used of him whose way of thinking, feeling, and acting is wholly conformed to the will of God, and who therefore needs no rectification in the heart or life; (1.a.3.a.) only Christ truly; (1.a.4.) approved of or acceptable of God; (1.b.) in a narrower sense, rendering to each his due and that in a judicial sense, passing just judgment on others, whether expressed in words or shown by the manner of dealing with them.

History provides many cases of rulers, kings, federal, state, and local government officials who have failed to conduct daily business in a just manner.

While there are those few who do conform to God's laws and commands, demonstrating their innocence, there are also those pseudo-Christians who take one verse out of context and base their entire denomination on that one verse. The New Testament is clear—one not approved or acceptable of God is not just.

They are simply people. They most likely go about their daily routine in a quiet, peaceful way, lovingly and compassionately doing what shows others who they are spiritually. They bear the fruit of the Spirit, which will be discussed in chapter 5.

- *Think on whatever is pure.*

When you think of the word *pure*, what comes to mind? Bottled water? Babies? Purity, as something upon which to think, can be a little more challenging than the others items. The key words are someone that excites (motivates) admiration, one that is respected, one free from concerns about the carnal,[14] one who is innocent, modest, faultless, clean and tidy, and spiritually clean. Sadly the most common group of people who fit these eloquent words are children, not adults!

The Greek definition for pure is *hagnos*: (1) exciting reverence (admiration), venerable, sacred; (2) Pure; (2.a.) pure from carnality, chaste, modest; (2.b.) pure from every fault, immaculate; (2.c.) clean (spiritually).

> But the wisdom from above is first pure, then peaceable, gentle, open to reason, full of mercy and good fruits, impartial and sincere. And a harvest of righteousness is sown in peace by those who make peace. (James 3:17–18)

---

[14] Webster: carnal: 1.a. relating to or given to crude bodily pleasures and appetites; b. marked by sexuality; 2. BODILY, CORPOREAL (seen with *carnal* eyes); 3.a. TEMPORAL (*carnal* weapons); b. WORLDLY (a *carnal* mind).

James explained the wisdom from above, talking about Jesus. Once more, the words easily describe both Jesus and little children. There is a reason for this connection.

> Then children were brought to him that he might lay his hands on them and pray. The disciples rebuked the people, but Jesus said, "Let the little children come to me and do not hinder them, for to such belongs the kingdom of heaven." (Matthew 19:13–14)

Real Christians model these characteristics as best they can, keeping in mind no human is perfect, with the understanding Christians are God's children.

> See what kind of love the Father has given to us, that we should be called children of God; and so we are. The reason why the world does not know us is that it did not know him. Beloved, we are God's children now, and what we will be has not yet appeared; but we know that when he appears we shall be like him, because we shall see him as he is. And everyone who thus hopes in him purifies himself as he is pure. (1 John 3:1–3)

As one thinks about the concept of being pure, and being a child of God, Christians must recall what was done to be in this pure state.

> Having purified your souls by your obedience to the truth for a sincere brotherly love, love one another earnestly from a pure heart, since you have been born again, not of perishable seed but of imperishable, through the living and abiding word of God. (1 Peter 1:22–23)

Real Christians purified their souls by obeying God, being born again through baptism, and then serving as living examples by following Jesus, the Word of God. As you think about purity, look for those you can identify who are spiritually pure, both as children and as adults.

- *Think on whatever is lovely.*

If you ask someone what they picture in their minds when they think about something that is lovely, they may say things like flowers, snow-covered mountains, flowing streams, colorful birds, schools of tropical fish around a coral reef, and ice cream in the summer!

The Greek definition of lovely is *prosphiles*: pleasing.

Things that one considers to be pleasing fall into three categories mentioned earlier: physical, emotional, spiritual. In the physical realm we use our sense of sight, hearing, smell, taste, and touch to recognize things we feel are pleasing or lovely. One caution, everything physical in the entire universe will be destroyed at the end of time, therefore nothing physical can be placed higher than our love of God.

> But the day of the Lord will come like a thief, and then the heavens will pass away with a roar, and the heavenly bodies will be burned up and dissolved, and the earth and the works that are done on it will be exposed. (2 Peter 3:10)

Things that one might believe to be emotionally pleasing could be the love of a parent, sibling, child, friend, or spouse. Others could include enjoying the presence of a dear friend or a playful pet. Positive humor can allow the brain to release endorphins which will quickly please the emotions through laughter.

Children frequently have a way with words as they learn how to talk. Parents have been known to keep a record of these sayings so they can share them later when the child is having a graduation party!

Spiritually, an answered prayer can be lovely. The real Christian routinely thanks God for each blessing provided, appreciative of the fact all blessings from God are good.

> Therefore I tell you, do not be anxious about your life, what you will eat or what you will drink, nor about your body, what you will put on. Is not life more than

food, and the body more than clothing? Look at the birds of the air: they neither sow nor reap nor gather into barns, and yet your heavenly Father feeds them. Are you not of more value than they? And which of you by being anxious can add a single hour to his span of life? And why are you anxious about clothing? Consider the lilies of the field, how they grow: they neither toil nor spin, yet I tell you, even Solomon in all his glory was not arrayed like one of these. But if God so clothes the grass of the field, which today is alive and tomorrow is thrown into the oven, will he not much more clothe you, O you of little faith? Therefore do not be anxious, saying, "What shall we eat?" or "What shall we drink?" or "What shall we wear?" For the Gentiles seek after all these things, and your heavenly Father knows that you need them all. But seek first the kingdom of God and his righteousness, and all these things will be added to you. Therefore do not be anxious about tomorrow, for tomorrow will be anxious for itself. Sufficient for the day is its own trouble. (Matthew 6:25–34)

Of the three—physical, emotional, and spiritual—the spiritual is most important. Jesus, in Matthew, tells real Christians to not be anxious about anything physical. God promises He will give His children, real Christians, what they need.

The guidance from Jesus is specific: seek first the kingdom of God and His righteousness—first, not second, third, or only on Sunday morning for an hour, first implies all the time, every day and night, from the time one's brain is mature enough to comprehend what is written in the New Testament[15] to when the person chooses to become a Christian, to the end of one's physical life here on earth.

● *Think on whatever is commendable.*

Mark Twain once said, "I can live for two months on a good compliment." Compliments, being spoken well of, having someone speak favorably about us, in most cases, is pleasing. People enjoy being commended for something they've accomplished. Business people, medical professionals, attorneys, auto mechanics, the military—all have a large selection of accoutrements on display. For many, framed degrees, diplomas, certificates of achievement, seminar attendance documents, or a large collection of recognizable initials after their name on a business card, are examples of inanimate items placed by one who hopes a visitor to their office will see them and compliment them. Auto mechanics and other blue-collar professionals place certificates on the walls where they work and frequently have several patches on their uniforms showing their credentials.

---

[15] Several medical studies in 2018 and 2019 indicate the human brain is fully formed and can logically process input without the interference of the sometimes irrational input from the frontal lobe around age twenty-five.

The military is known for service ribbons/medals, medals for combat service and heroism, and pins showing specialty training accomplishments.

Napoleon once said, "A soldier will fight long and hard for a bit of colored ribbon."

The Greek word for commendable is *euphemos*: (1) sounding well; (2) uttering words of good omen, speaking auspiciously (favorably).

Many times, one will become discouraged and frustrated when their work is seldom, if ever, appreciated by the "boss." "I didn't get the promotion I wanted." "I didn't get the raise I deserved." What is the result when a group of friends meet for a social event, and "Nobody said anything about my new shoes?"

Real Christians have a different outlook on this life. They know they may work quietly and never receive any positive human feedback on the results. When they do receive a compliment, spiritually they look at a compliment as a reward for their faith-based actions. Real Christians are humble, a concept discussed later. Real Christians look for opportunities to commend, compliment, and praise others.

> And let us not grow weary of doing good, for in due season we will reap, if we do not give up. So then, as we have opportunity, let us do good to everyone, and especially to those who are of the household of faith. (Galatians 6:9–10)

Real Christians do not wait for their opportunity to come knocking on their front door. They do everything they can to become an opportunity for all others.

Real Christians do not give up easily. Why?

> I can do all things through him who strengthens me. (Philippians 4:13)

During his presidential campaign, Abraham Lincoln was about to face an opponent in a debate. The public knew the two men did not agree on much of anything, but when a reporter asked Lincoln what he thought about the other man, he replied, "I don't like that man. I must get to know him better." Real Christians work at getting to know others so they can commend them and encourage them to study, learn, think, and choose to become a Christian too. Remember, everyone has something to do in this life, even if at first their only purpose seems to be serving as a bad example!

- *Think on whatever is excellent.*

Some synonyms for "excellent" are merit, perfection, quality, virtue, value, worth, distinction, fineness, superiority, goodness, niceness. In the physical world, those who are looked at as being excellent are certain athletes who win gold medals, those who are recognized for helping others in a public way, perhaps by buying a family a new home after a disaster or someone who retires after forty years with the same company.

The Greek definition for excellence is *arete*: (1) a virtuous course of thought, feeling and action; (1.a.) virtue, moral goodness; (2) any particular moral excellence, as modesty, purity.

Real Christians must look at excellence from a spiritual point of view.

Notice these words from the Greek: virtuous course of thought, moral goodness, modesty, purity. Winning a gold medal has little to do with virtue, moral goodness, or modesty. Helping any human being in any way possible at any time throughout the life of a Christian can be defined as excellent. In what ways can we identify one who is excellent?

> But as you excel in everything—in faith, in speech, in knowledge, in all earnestness, and in our love for you—see that you excel in this act of grace also. I say this not as a command, but to prove by the earnestness of others that your love also is genuine. (2 Corinthians 8:7–8)

Paul provided yet another list of opportunities for real Christians to include in their thoughts and actions each day. In addition to identifying those who demonstrate these characteristics, ask yourself, "What am I doing to be excellent in these areas?"

● *Think on anything worthy of praise.*

The challenge is to think about anything worthy of praise. Praise of children is much more than a parent repeating the statement "good job!" fifty times a day.

"Oh, you looked out the window! Good job!" "Oh, you sat in a chair! Good job" "Wow! You looked out the window again! Good job!" This phony praise conditions children to expect this feedback from everyone all the time. Then when children go to school and are not praised every time they blink their eyes, they become confused and begin to wonder if something is wrong with them.

The Greek definition for praise is *epainos*: approbation (approval, admiration), commendation, praise.

Working adults who receive a paper certificate showing they once again sat through a one-day training program then frame it and hang it on their cubicle wall are quite common. What is less common is for their supervisor to follow up on the training program by waiting three months, then having a conversation with the employee to see if there have been any improvements in performance directly related to the material covered. If the person has learned and is practicing the lessons offered, a good supervisor will then offer the deserved praise to the employee.

Military men and women who complete basic training come home on leave wearing their dress uniforms. They proudly wear a red and yellow striped ribbon on their chest. What excellent task did they complete to earn this medal? They joined the military. The award, the National Defense Service Medal, is given automatically just for signing up and finishing basic training. Once more, some fall into the physical and emotional trap where superficial, shallow, or completely insignificant approvals, commendations, or praise takes priority over spiritual wealth.

The real Christian thinks about, and searches for, people, methods, procedures, and Scripture that clarify excellence from God's point of view. If it is difficult to identify a person right now, there is another option!

> Praise the Lord! Praise God in his sanctuary; praise him in his mighty heavens! Praise him for his mighty deeds; praise him according to his excellent greatness! (Psalm 150:1–2)

As one who stands looking into the closet, thinking about what to wear, the real Christian knows thinking is not the end of the journey. The decision to put on the proper attire must be followed by really working to put on the best God has provided.

Chapter 3 questions and challenges

1. What time of day do you do your best thinking? Do you have a quiet place free from distractions where you can think about the concepts presented in this chapter? Distractions include phones, televisions, radios, and other electronic devices that can pull one's attention away from thinking.

2. Remember the definition of thinking (*logizomai*): (1) reason about, ponder, think about; (2) keep mental record, bear in mind; (3) hold a view, have an opinion.
3. As you invest your mind in thinking about the topics presented, plan for enough time to ponder, then form an opinion based on the Scripture used in this chapter.

CHAPTER 4

THOSE WHO PUT ON...

> If conversion to Christianity makes no improvement in a man's outward actions—if he continues to be just as snobbish or spiteful or envious or ambitious as he was before—then I think we must suspect that his "conversion" was largely imaginary.
>
> —C. S. Lewis, *Mere Christianity*

Paul provided a wonderful collection of spiritual things real Christians can wear. Real Christians believe it begins with putting on Jesus via baptism.

> Now before faith came, we were held captive under the law, imprisoned until the coming faith would be revealed. So then, the law was our guardian until Christ came, in order that we might be justified by faith. But now that faith has

> come, we are no longer under a guardian, for in Christ Jesus you are all sons of God, through faith. For as many of you as were baptized into Christ have put on Christ. There is neither Jew nor Greek, there is neither slave nor free, there is no male and female, for you are all one in Christ Jesus. And if you are Christ's, then you are Abraham's offspring, heirs according to promise. (Galatians 3:23–29)

The act of putting something on always includes action. To put on a coat, the body must move and contort to put arms into sleeves, then fingers must manipulate buttons into button holes.

The Greek word for "put on" is *enduō*: clothe, dress (another); dress oneself, wear clothes.

> Put on then, as God's chosen ones, holy and beloved, compassionate hearts, kindness, humility, meekness, and patience, bearing with one another and, if one has a complaint against another, forgiving each other; as the Lord has forgiven you, so you also must forgive. And above all these put on love, which binds everything together in perfect harmony. And let the peace of Christ rule in your hearts, to which indeed you were called in one body. And be thankful. (Colossians 3:12–15)

After reading the list of things real Christians are to put on, these characteristics will also help one who is not a Christian recognize those who are. If any of these distinct characteristics are missing, one must question the belief, faith, and legitimacy of the one being analyzed and observed.

- *Put on a compassionate heart.*

Someone may say, "I feel it in my heart," not meaning there is something physical taking place in the fist-sized pump under our ribs but something emotional. Purists will state there is a big difference between the brain and the heart, but those in the know easily grasp the mind-body connection. The brain cannot function without being connected to the body; and conversely, the body cannot function without being connected to the brain.

The Greek word for compassion is *oiktirmos*: (1) compassion, pity, mercy; (1.a.) bowels in which compassion resides, a heart of compassion; (1.b.) emotions, longings, manifestations of pity.

Heart in Greek is *splagchnon*: (1) bowels, intestines, (the heart, lungs, liver, etc.); (1.a.) bowels; (1.b.) the bowels were regarded as the seat of the more violent passions, such as anger and love; but by the Hebrews as the seat of the more tender affections, esp. kindness, benevolence, compassion; hence our heart (tender mercies, affections, etc.); (1.c.) a heart in which mercy resides.

Our last topic was about thinking on certain things. As real Christians reason, ponder, and spend time praying and studying the life of Jesus, they can begin the process of comprehending what is meant by "put these on." As with thinking on certain things, putting on this next list is also a lifelong process of learning and growth. Interestingly, these are all connected because they all affect the physical, emotional, and spiritual parts of our presence here and with other real Christians on the planet.

- *Put on kindness.*

Real Christians demonstrate kindness with no concern for praise or commendation from others. Real Christians can easily be kind without anyone else knowing who was behind the kindness. One example is paying for the meal of someone you don't know when you pay for your own meal and then quickly leave the restaurant. Another is paying the toll for the person behind you when going through a toll booth.

The Greek word for kindness is *chrestotes*: (1) moral goodness, integrity; (2) benignity, kindness.

The Greek definition of the word kindness includes "integrity." It has been said, the difference between integrity and honesty is that telling the truth to others is honesty, while telling the truth to yourself is integrity. Benignity means doing kind actions with gentleness. One example is a driver who keeps a new bottle of water and a twenty-dollar bill in the car. Then when at a red light and a beggar comes to the window, instead of ignoring the one looking for help, the Christian will smile, roll the window down, and give the person the water and the money. Some will say, "When you give a beggar money, they're just going to go buy drugs or alcohol." That may be true but can also mean the person can buy food for a child. When a gift is given in love, the giver knows it is now up to the one receiving the gift to decide what to do. Jesus gave His life for all humanity. And since that time, it is up to individuals to either decide to follow Him or walk away. He gave this perfect gift without conditions.

Real Christians do the same and pray for good results. One additional reason to show kindness to others is this:

> Let brotherly love continue. Do not neglect to show hospitality to strangers, for thereby some have entertained angels unawares. (Hebrews 13:1–2)

Be kind because of your love for humanity. You may not really know who is at the other end of your kindness. It might be an angel!

● *Put on humility.*

Take a moment and read this passage out loud:

> Do nothing from rivalry or conceit, but in humility count others more significant than yourselves. Let each of you look not only to his own interests, but also to the interests of others. Have this mind among yourselves, which is yours in Christ Jesus,

> who, though he was in the form of God, did not count equality with God a thing to be grasped, but made himself nothing, taking the form of a servant, being born in the likeness of men. And being found in human form, he humbled himself by becoming obedient to the point of death, even death on a cross. (Philippians 2:3–8)

The Greek definition of the word humility is *tapeinophrosune*: (1) having a humble opinion of one's self; (2) a deep sense of one's (moral) littleness; (3) modesty, humility, lowliness of mind.

When we think about Jesus and His life, He never identified Himself as more important, more valuable, more powerful, or more significant than those He came to save. He was the true servant, even to the point of His physical death. One identifier of a real Christian is the readiness to count others as more important, more valuable, in need of love and compassion, and eagerness to do everything possible to be an example to others, even to the point of dying. Jesus said, "This is my commandment, that you love one another as I have loved you. Greater love has no one than this, that someone lay down his life for his friends. You are my friends if you do what I command you" (John 15:12–14).

Here, Jesus commanded that we love unconditionally, even to the point of dying. There are many accounts of civilians, military, volunteers, medical staff, etc. who, while doing their work, sacrificed themselves without hesitation to save the life of another. One may ask, "What would I do in that situation?" Each individual must answer that question when and if placed in a similar situation. All else is pure speculation.

Real Christians can be identified by what they do, but it's also imperative we look at what they do not do. They don't talk about themselves very much, and they don't demonstrate false bravado. Real Christians don't draw attention to themselves when they are doing those things pleasing to God, and they don't brag about what they've done in the past. Real Christians don't demean any non-Christian. Instead, they see every person as a potential Christian and, for that reason, will never advocate for the physical destruction of another human life. Never!

- *Put on meekness.*

Meekness does not mean cowardice. The Greek word for meek is *praus*: mildness of disposition, gentleness of spirit, meekness.

Additional information: Gentleness or meekness is the opposite to self-assertiveness and self-interest. It stems from trust in God's goodness and control over the situation. The gentle person is not occupied with self at all. This is a work of the Holy Spirit, not of the human will. (Note: The word *coward* is not found in the New Testament.)

From the 1930 *Webster's Dictionary*:

Meek: gentle; submissive; yielding; mild of temper

Notice the similarities with the addition of submissive and being mild of temper.

Pseudo-Christians have different emotional masks they wear for different occasions. On Sunday morning in the worship building, they wear a smiling mask.

They shake hands and talk about the weather. They bow their head lower than the others in the same pew during a prayer. They carry a Bible, but the dust shows it is never opened and probably sits on the back seat of the car all week until the next Sunday. They sing as loud as they can, looking around to see if anyone notices how religious they are acting. (Note: The key word here is "*acting*!") On Monday morning, they put on their work mask. This mask doesn't smile much, curses other drivers for being either too fast or too slow. This mask waits for two or three cups of coffee to "get the day going." When they come home, they put on the "I had a terrible day at work" mask, hoping for sympathy from their spouse, the kids, or the dog who is always happy to see anyone. After dinner, they put on the "I am only interested in watching sports tonight, so don't even look at me!" mask.

And so it goes.

Real Christians do not have masks. They do not camouflage their feelings or actions. What you see and hear is what you get. Period.

Some may think being submissive is a negative reaction to any given situation. Our perfect example, Jesus, began by being submissive to His parents.

> After three days they found him in the temple, sitting among the teachers, listening to them and asking them questions.

> And all who heard him were amazed at his understanding and his answers. And when his parents saw him, they were astonished. And his mother said to him, "Son, why have you treated us so? Behold, your father and I have been searching for you in great distress." And he said to them, "Why were you looking for me? Did you not know that I must be in my Father's house?" And they did not understand the saying that he spoke to them. And he went down with them and came to Nazareth and was submissive to them. And his mother treasured up all these things in her heart. And Jesus increased in wisdom and in stature and in favor with God and man. (Luke 2:46–52)

From the 1930 *Webster's Dictionary*: Submissive means yielding to authority; obedient; humble.

The real Christian is compliant with federal, state, and local laws, so long as they do not violate Jesus's commands. While Jesus never involved Himself in politics, He was clear about this:

> Tell us, then, what you think. Is it lawful to pay taxes to Caesar, or not?" But Jesus, aware of their malice, said, "Why put me to the test, you hypocrites? Show me the coin for the tax." And they brought him a denarius. And Jesus said

to them, "Whose likeness and inscription is this?" They said, "Caesar's." Then he said to them, "Therefore render to Caesar the things that are Caesar's, and to God the things that are God's." (Matthew 22:17–21)

Paul wrote:

> For because of this you also pay taxes, for the authorities are ministers of God, attending to this very thing. Pay to all what is owed to them: taxes to whom taxes are owed, revenue to whom revenue is owed, respect to whom respect is owed, honor to whom honor is owed. (Romans 13:6–7)

One lesson in these verses that is often overlooked is, that people in positions of leadership and power are in place because of the power of God. As such, they are to be obeyed. Soldiers learning how to march must be meek (submissive/obedient) to their drill instructor. Orchestras must be meek (submissive/obedient) to the conductor. All pilots must be meek (submissive/obedient) to the law of gravity! (Just kidding.)

The questions real Christians must answer are, "For what purpose am I putting on all these things? Why do I have to be meek?" Have patience, and keep reading!

● *Put on patience.*

Some have said, "God, give me patience and give it to me now!" "Jesus came over two thousand years ago. When is He coming back to take us away from this insanity?" Or a parent may say, "Don't make me come in there!" And one more: "I have one nerve left, and you're getting on it!"

The Greek definition of patience is *makrothumia*: (1) patience, endurance, constancy, steadfastness, perseverance; (2) patience, forbearance, longsuffering, slowness in avenging wrongs.

Physical patience means accepting the human body has certain limitations.

With proper training and exercise, one may be able to run a marathon or swim a mile in record time. With little or no training, running more than ten feet from the recliner to the kitchen is more challenging than a marathon. With increasing age, there is a corresponding decrease in physical ability. Real Christians are patient with themselves as they age physically because they recognize there is a trade-off taking place.

When the physical strength, hearing, eyesight, and the other senses fade, the spiritual part of the person is growing, preparing for life eternal in heaven. Life is a balancing act. The physical weakens while the spiritual strengthens. Instead of hoping for a drug, an exercise or diet, plastic surgery, Botox, or some new clinical science to extend life all while making one more beautiful or handsome in the process, real Christians focus on spiritually moving closer to God.

Emotional patience means accepting people—both children and adults—are all different with a wide variety of wants and needs. Violence against children is most often a lack of patience on the part of a parent, grandparent, or other family member tasked with providing care for the child. A child's cry is a simple nonverbal request for a need to be filled: food, a clean diaper, or just wanting to be held close to another warm body!

Road rage frequently makes the news. One remedy is to acknowledge we rarely know other drivers on the road, where they are going, what their purpose for driving is, and where they are physically, emotionally, or spiritually in their lives.

Instead of labeling the other driver as "too fast," "too slow," "stupid," or "a fool," consider saying this short prayer: "God, that person in front of me is driving in a careless manner. Please allow them to arrive safely at their destination without harming themselves or another person, in Jesus's name, amen."

Spiritual patience means looking at the example Jesus provides in the New Testament.

> First of all, then, I urge that supplications, prayers, intercessions, and thanksgivings be made for all people, for kings and all who are in high positions, that we may lead a peaceful and quiet life, godly and dignified in every way. This is good, and it is pleasing in the sight of God our Savior, who desires all people to be saved

and to come to the knowledge of the truth. (1 Timothy 2:1–4)

God desires all people to be saved! Given human nature and the mass confusion caused by the denominational world, combined with atheists, agnostics, and other false teachers, this is going to take some time. The real Christian knows the control of this is in the hands of God, not humans.

Many citizens of countries all around the world become impatient when their government leaders do things that anger or frustrate them. Revolutions, uprisings, protests, and wars are the result. But look at the first part of this passage. Real Christians pray for all people, for kings, and other government leaders so that "we (real Christians) may lead a peaceful and quiet life, godly and dignified in every way." Praying that we, as real Christians, may lead lives that are peaceful, quiet, godly, and dignified automatically excludes all things that are the opposite.

These include, but are not limited to, violent acts instead of peaceful; loud, unruly, and boisterous behaviors instead of quiet; ungodly irreverent, disrespectful, ill-mannered, and discourteous actions instead of godly; improper, demeaning, offensive, debasing, critical, hateful, and inappropriate actions instead of being dignified. If there is anyone who claims to be a Christian and their actions show one or more of these negative characteristics, their validity as a Christian must be questioned.

So-called religious leaders who argue for war, patriotism, nationalism, waving the flag, and encouraging

America—that Christian nation—to kill, torture, or severely punish anyone who is not a Christian have forgotten or never really recognized one thing:

> For many, of whom I have often told you and now tell you even with tears, walk as enemies of the cross of Christ. Their end is destruction, their god is their belly, and they glory in their shame, with minds set on earthly things. But our citizenship is in heaven, and from it we await a Savior, the Lord Jesus Christ, who will transform our lowly body to be like his glorious body, by the power that enables him even to subject all things to himself. (Philippians 3:18–21)

Those screaming for war and destruction are enemies of Jesus! They focus on the physical—their belly, their shame (often labeled abuse of power and out-of-control ego) and live only for earthly things. Real Christians unmistakably are not concerned about their earthly passport or place of birth but know their true and most-important citizenship is in heaven. Christians have no flag or national anthem.

Christians, when they put on patience, remember that another part of this process is putting on love!

> Hatred stirs up strife, but love covers all offenses. (Proverbs 10:12)

> The end of all things is at hand; therefore be self-controlled and sober-minded for the sake of your prayers. Above all, keep loving one another earnestly, since love covers a multitude of sins. (1 Peter 4:7–8)

The reaction of the real Christians is to be self-controlled, clear-headed, self-restrained, all while praying for others, and then allowing love to move one past the fear, anger, and hate that result from being impatient. The most common result of fear, anger, and hate is the injury or death of another human. No real Christian would assume to be the judge of other humans, killing them, and removing the possibility of them learning about God and His Word. That is not a patient attitude, and it certainly is not a Christian's attitude!

- *Put on the willingness to bear with another.*

Real Christians are the family and children of God:

> You are my friends if you do what I command you. No longer do I call you servants, for the servant does not know what his master is doing; but I have called you friends, for all that I have heard from my Father I have made known to you. (John 15:14–15)

The family of real Christians love each other and spiritually support them for the duration of their lives. They think about each other. They are stubborn in their support for each other. They care.

Bearing in Greek means *anechomai*: (1) to hold up; (2) to hold one's self erect and firm; (3) to sustain, to bear, to endure.

Another in Greek means *allelon*: one another, reciprocally, mutually.

Bearing is frequently combined with patience. Bearing with another person goes beyond patience in that it includes physical, emotional, and spiritual support.

A gentle hug, a kind word, and a thoughtful prayer come to mind.

> I therefore, a prisoner for the Lord, urge you to walk in a manner worthy of the calling to which you have been called, with all humility and gentleness, with patience, bearing with one another in love, eager to maintain the unity of the Spirit in the bond of peace. (Ephesians 4:1–3)

A real Christian will never give up on another person even when they feel it isn't worth caring anymore. Jesus, in His weakest physical moment, gave us the perfect reply:

> And when they came to the place that is called The Skull, there they crucified him, and the criminals, one on his

right and one on his left. And Jesus said, "Father, forgive them, for they know not what they do." (Luke 23:33–34a)

- *Put on forgiveness.*

John F. Kennedy said, "Forgive your enemies but never forget their name."

His comment was meant to bring a smile; but obviously, it is not in line with God's view.

The Greek word for forgive is *charizomai*: (1) to do something pleasant or agreeable (to one), to do a favor to, gratify; (1.a.) to show one's self gracious, kind, benevolent; (1.b.) to grant forgiveness, to pardon; (1.c.) to give graciously, give freely, bestow; (1.c.1.) to forgive; (1.c.2.) graciously to restore one to another; (1.c.3.) to preserve for one a person in peril.

We humans can forgive but seldom forget what the other person did to us.

Perhaps the Eskimo's nation's language can help. When the Moravian missionaries first went to the Eskimos[16], they could not find a word in their language for forgiveness, so they had to compound one. This turned out to be *issumagijoujungnainermik*. It is a formidable-looking assembly of letters but an expression that has a beautiful connotation for those who understand it. It means "not being able to think about it anymore."[17]

---

[16] 1732, The Moravians originated in Bohemia.
[17] Paul Lee Tan, *Encyclopedia of 7700 Illustrations: A Treasury of Illustrations, Anecdotes, Facts and Quotations for Pastors, Teachers and Christian Workers* (Garland TX: Bible Communications, 1996, c1979).

What a perfect way to think about forgiveness! Don't think about it anymore! Let me clarify that statement. The word *don't* is not an effective command. If I say, "Don't look at my mismatched socks," what will a normal person do? Look at the socks! The Eskimos say it much better: "I am not able to think about it anymore."

The real Christian forgives and, because of knowing God does not remember forgiven sins, will say, "I will not think about it anymore." This requires a sense of learning and practicing the focus on more positive thinking. Practice rarely makes perfect, but it does improve our ability to forgive. Real Christians are not perfect, but they are forgiven!

> But when Christ had offered for all time a single sacrifice for sins, he sat down at the right hand of God, waiting from that time until his enemies should be made a footstool for his feet. For by a single offering he has perfected for all time those who are being sanctified. And the Holy Spirit also bears witness to us; for after saying, "This is the covenant that I will make with them after those days, declares the Lord: I will put my laws on their hearts, and write them on their minds," then he adds, "I will remember their sins and their lawless deeds no more." Where there is forgiveness of these, there is no longer any offering for sin. (Hebrews 10:12–18)

This does not mean a Christian will never sin after becoming a member of the family of God. Real Christians know that if they refuse to forgive another person, it is sin. They also recognize that if they truly know what exact action is needed in any situation and do not do that action, it is sin.

> So whoever knows the right thing
> to do and fails to do it, for him it is sin.
> (James 4:17)

Many new Christians who have not had follow-up teaching and coaching on examples of the right thing to do, can easily struggle to the point where they shake their heads and walk away from God. For the reader, this is a critical reminder that everything we are discussing in this book is all part of the process of growing into a mature, real Christian. There is much to think about; there is much to put on. And following that, there is much to do!

Not listed in these verses about "putting on" but equally important is the following:

> Finally, be strong in the Lord and in the strength of his might. Put on the whole armor of God, that you may be able to stand against the schemes of the devil. For we do not wrestle against flesh and blood, but against the rulers, against the authorities, against the cosmic powers over this present darkness, against the spiritual forces of evil in the heavenly places. Therefore

> take up the whole armor of God, that you may be able to withstand in the evil day, and having done all, to stand firm. Stand therefore, having fastened on the belt of truth, and having put on the breastplate of righteousness, and, as shoes for your feet, having put on the readiness given by the gospel of peace. In all circumstances take up the shield of faith, with which you can extinguish all the flaming darts of the evil one; and take the helmet of salvation, and the sword of the Spirit, which is the word of God, praying at all times in the Spirit, with all prayer and supplication. To that end keep alert with all perseverance, making supplication (prayers) for all the saints. (Ephesians 6:10–18)

- *Put on love.*

Finally, real Christians put on love so it can pull everything together in perfect harmony. Putting love on is a multifaceted journey that begins with loving oneself.

> "Teacher, which is the great commandment in the Law?" And he said to him, "You shall love the Lord your God with all your heart and with all your soul and with all your mind. This is the great and first commandment. And a second

is like it: You shall love your neighbor as yourself." (Matthew 22:36–39)

Jesus is crystal clear in His reply to the question. The first part is *the* great and *first* commandment. Real Christians study and work hard to love God *completely*. It takes priority over any earthly, physical desire. The words heart, soul, and mind are prefaced with "all." The Greek word for all is *holos*: all, whole, completely.

All means all, and whole means whole, and completely means completely!

Being a real Christian is not a part-time job. It is a full-time joy! Being a real Christian is so much more than a dusty Bible in the back seat of the car that is taken into the building on Sunday morning. It is more than one telling others, "Yes, I am religious because I have a Bible, and I go to church on Sunday morning, Sunday evening, and also go to the Wednesday evening Bible study. And I also have a 'Honk If You Love Jesus's bumper sticker on my car."

The second and equally important part of Jesus's reply is to love your neighbor as yourself. Some in the denominational world falsely argue one's neighbor means only other Christians. Because of this opinion, pseudo-Christians feel justified when they advocate the killing of anyone who is not a Christian. At the time of this writing, 2019–2020, the Western Christian community believes it is at war with anyone in the Muslim faith, illegal immigrants, the Russians, anyone who does not have an American flag hanging outside their house, and the list goes on and on. The obvious question is, "Where is the love Jesus commanded His followers to have?" The love isn't there because of a lack of understanding how Jesus defined a neighbor.

The Greek word for neighbor is *plesion*: (1) a neighbor; (1.a.) a friend; (1.b.) any other person, and where two are concerned, the other (thy fellow man, thy neighbor), according to the Jews, any member of the Hebrew race and commonwealth; (1.c.) according to Christ, any other man irrespective of ethnicity or religion with whom we live or whom we chance to meet.

Those of the Jewish faith still believe their neighbor is simply another Jew who believes like they do. Like Christian denominations, there are also an assortment of Jewish denominations.

Jesus looks at any human, those sharing space on the earth, those we may meet face-to-face at any time, as a neighbor. The 1930 *Webster's Dictionary* defines neighbor as one who dwells near to another; an intimate; near to another; adjacent; to adjoin (connect to); to be neighborly or friendly.

One not interested in enthusiastically loving their neighbor will claim, "Those heathens on the other side of the world can't be my neighbor because I can physically see the houses of my neighbors where I live!" From a universal, spiritual perspective, this argument is invalid. When looking at photographs of our solar system, we say "neighboring planets, stars, galaxies," etc. to describe parts of creation that we can and cannot see. Jesus states that if there is another human on this planet earth, that person is a neighbor.

The more important part of His reply is found in the second part of verse 39.

We must love our self too! While there may not be any scientific studies on this topic, I believe most of the fear, hate, anger, and struggle for power over others come directly from the fact that so many people do not love themselves. One easy test to validate my point of view is this: Can you, right now, go look into a mirror and say to yourself, "I love you"? Loving all of humanity does not mean accepting the evil actions some do out of hate. It simply means loving the soul of that person in the hope they will have an opportunity to learn about Jesus and His plan of salvation for all humans. It means searching for ways to teach others so that the bad is replaced with the good. There is much more about love that will be discussed in the next chapter.

Chapter 4 questions and challenges

1. If you haven't already done so, go stand in front of a mirror and say, "I love you." How did it feel? What did your face look like? What were you thinking? If you are a Christian, was there ever a time in your past where loving yourself was identified as being so important? When? Why?
2. When you first wake up tomorrow morning, take a moment to determine which of the items in this chapter you will put on. Just as with getting physically dressed, put on one thing at a time. Get comfortable with your new spiritual attire. Adjust it until you can easily go out in public and be the example God wants you to be. Oh, and talk to the mirror!

CHAPTER 5

Those Who Actively Demonstrate Fruits of the Spirit

A person learns to swim in the water, not in the library.

—Paulo Freire

We are now at the point where everything we've looked at before this chapter falls into place and is the basis for the ultimate examples of real Christians doing what they do. Like a small child growing up and preparing to attend school, the new Christian has done the same on a spiritual level. Having been taught, having obeyed the Word of God, having thought about Christian concepts, having been dressed with the necessary spiritual clothing, it is now time to go to work!

> But the fruit of the Spirit is love, joy, peace, patience, kindness, goodness, faithfulness, gentleness, self-control; against such things there is no law. And those who belong to Christ Jesus have crucified the flesh with its passions and desires. If we live by the Spirit, let us also walk by the Spirit. (Galatians 5:22–25)

Before examining the fruits of the Spirit, we will look at what the Holy Spirit actually does for the real Christian. We mentioned earlier about receiving a gift—remember the cookies promised by a mother? Exactly what does the New Testament show us about the actions of the Holy Spirit? Our first clue is the Holy Spirit fills and governs our soul. The Holy Spirit can be defined as the third person of the trinity, the God, the Holy Spirit, the disposition or influence which fills and governs the soul of anyone.[18]

If the Holy Spirit fills and governs our souls, how does that process take place? First, one must love Jesus and keep His commandments. Once that has taken place, God will give that Christian a Helper who will be with that person forever. The gift of the Holy Spirit is not the power for anyone to do miraculous acts, to instantaneously speak in

---

[18] James Strong, *The Exhaustive Concordance of the Bible: Showing Every Word of the Text of the Common English Version of the Canonical Books, and Every Occurrence of Each Word in Regular Order*, electronic ed., G4151 (Ontario: Woodside Bible Fellowship, 1996).

another language, or to tell the future. The cookie promised by the mother provided nourishment when it entered the body. The Holy Spirit provides help once it enters the soul of the Christian.

> If you love me, you will keep my commandments. And I will ask the Father, and he will give you another Helper, to be with you forever, even the Spirit of truth, whom the world cannot receive, because it neither sees him nor knows him. You know him, for he dwells with you and will be in you. (John 14:15–17)

What must be done that will allow God to put the Holy Spirit into one's soul? Repent and be baptized.

> Let all the house of Israel therefore know for certain that God has made him both Lord and Christ, this Jesus whom you crucified." Now when they heard this they were cut to the heart, and said to Peter and the rest of the apostles, "Brothers, what shall we do?" And Peter said to them, "Repent and be baptized every one of you in the name of Jesus Christ for the forgiveness of your sins, and you will receive the gift of the Holy Spirit. (Acts 2:36–38)

The Holy Spirit is a gift from God only after one makes the choice to show obedience to God by becoming a Christian.

> But Peter and the apostles answered, "We must obey God rather than men. The God of our fathers raised Jesus, whom you killed by hanging him on a tree. God exalted him at his right hand as Leader and Savior, to give repentance to Israel and forgiveness of sins. And we are witnesses to these things, and so is the Holy Spirit, whom God has given to those who obey him." (Acts 5:29–32)

With the sacrifice Jesus made for all humans, the physical, emotional, and spiritual body of that person who has obeyed God is no longer hers. She was bought by Jesus.

> Or do you not know that your body is a temple of the Holy Spirit within you, whom you have from God? You are not your own, for you were bought with a price. So glorify God in your body. (1 Corinthians 6:19–20)

The new body is now a temple for the Holy Spirit. The Greek word for temple is *naos*: used of the temple at Jerusalem but only of the sacred edifice (or sanctuary) itself, consisting of the Holy place and the Holy of Holies (in classical Greek, it is used of the sanctuary or cell of the temple where the image of gold was placed, which is distinguished from the whole enclosure).

If the Christian's body is now a spiritual temple or "holy place" containing the Holy Spirit, the real Christian strongly behaves in a manner that always glorifies God. As mentioned before, this means more than the brief visit to the worship building for one or two hours each week. This is a daily collection of accomplishments as the result of fulfilling the obligations of being a Christian. For those real Christians who are chronologically older than their younger Christian friends, they know there are times when their soul is tired, weak, and exhausted from the daily battle with the evil powers of the devil. God thought of that, and this is the next benefit of being a child of God. We have help!

> Likewise the Spirit helps us in our weakness. For we do not know what to pray for as we ought, but the Spirit himself intercedes for us with groanings too deep for words. And he who searches hearts knows what is the mind of the Spirit, because the Spirit intercedes for the saints according to the will of God. (Romans 8:26–27)

Real Christians do not spend unfruitful time preparing lengthy, wordy prayers designed to impress others. Straightforward, uncomplicated prayers work because the

Holy Spirit takes our prayers and translates them so that God can hear and answer them.

Finally, the Holy Spirit teaches us through our study of the Bible. King David wrote:

> Create in me a clean heart, O God, and renew a right spirit within me. Cast me not away from your presence, and take not your Holy Spirit from me. Restore to me the joy of your salvation, and uphold me with a willing spirit. Then I will teach transgressors your ways, and sinners will return to you. (Psalm 51:10–13)

It is perfectly okay to take David's words in verses 10 through 12 and use them as a simple prayer to God. Verse 13 is a good lesson for what to do after that prayer has been answered: Teach others! Remember John 14:15–16a: "If you love me, you will keep my commandments. And I will ask the Father, and he will give you another Helper, to be with you forever."

The seed has been planted. It has been fed through Bible study and prayer. It is now time to enjoy and share the fruit.

● *Those who actively demonstrate love*

The Greek word *agape* means brotherly love, affection, good will, love, benevolence.

In the original Greek, from the time of the writing of the New Testament, there were four words for "love." Agape, or brotherly love, is the most common in the New Testament. *Storge* means love of family. *Phileo* means love of friends.

Finally, *eros* is sexual love. *Eros* is not used in the New Testament.

The type of love shown to humanity by Jesus is agape love. The words used in the definition are self-explanatory. The most famous and one of the most important passages in the New Testament that talks about love is this:

> If I speak in the tongues of men and of angels, but have not love, I am a noisy gong or a clanging cymbal. And if I have prophetic powers, and understand all mysteries and all knowledge, and if I have all faith, so as to remove mountains, but have not love, I am nothing. If I give away all I have, and if I deliver up my body to be burned, but have not love, I gain nothing. Love is patient and kind; love does not envy or boast; it is not arrogant or rude. It does not insist on its own way; it is not irritable or resentful; it does not rejoice at wrongdoing, but rejoices with the truth. Love bears all things, believes all things, hopes all things, endures all things. Love never ends. As for prophecies, they will pass away; as for tongues, they will cease;

as for knowledge, it will pass away. For we know in part and we prophesy in part, but when the perfect comes, the partial will pass away. When I was a child, I spoke like a child, I thought like a child, I reasoned like a child. When I became a man, I gave up childish ways. For now we see in a mirror dimly, but then face to face. Now I know in part; then I shall know fully, even as I have been fully known. So now faith, hope, and love abide, these three; but the greatest of these is love. (1 Corinthians 13:1–13)

This is the encyclopedia of agape love, and it takes a lifetime of practice, experimenting, successes and failures, determination, and endurance as the real Christian moves toward the ultimate goal of doing everything possible to replicate the love of God for humanity. Spiritually, real Christians live for (and with) faith, hope, and love. Note: Don't forget to look in the mirror and say, "I love you!"

- *Those who actively demonstrate joy*

Can joy be faked? Some, in the denominational world, appear to ignore sincere human emotions. One denomination has a Sunday morning television program where the congregation sings together on camera. The preacher, with a big smile on his face and is never seen in the congregation but on a separate set designed to look like an office, announces the group will be worshipping in song.

As the camera pans across the auditorium, something seems a little out of place.

Reflected in the glasses of those singing are multiple sets of bright spotlights.

Every single person is holding a songbook, but most are obviously reading the words on the giant screen at the front of the auditorium. Many are not smiling at all until the camera happens to be right in front of them, and then magically a smile appears! The group is packed tightly together to give the impression the room is full of worshippers. Strangely, there are no babies, toddlers, or young children in the group. The group is focused on a song leader who, while not on camera, has clearly instructed the group to overemphasize their pronunciation of the words. It gives the impression many are singing in fear of making a mistake. Sadly, it is obvious the group singing is staged. This is not joy. This is ritualized tradition.

The Greek word for joy is *chara*: (1) joy, gladness; (1.a.) the joy received from you; (1.b.) the cause or occasion of joy; (1.b.1.) of persons who are one's joy.

Real Christians are glad to be in the presence of God when worshipping together. They smile because of the occasion of joy being in the presence of God.

They also delight in seeing another person being baptized or in knowing an errant Christian has returned and asked forgiveness of God.

> What man of you, having a hundred sheep, if he has lost one of them, does not leave the ninety-nine in the open country, and go after the one that is lost, until he finds it? And when he has found it, he lays it on his shoulders, rejoicing. And when he comes home, he calls together his friends and his neighbors, saying to them, "Rejoice with me, for I have found my sheep that was lost." Just so, I tell you, there will be more joy in heaven over one sinner who repents than over ninety-nine righteous persons who need no repentance. (Luke 15:4–7)

Joy is not raucous laughter, silly actions, wild and erratic behavior, telling jokes, or being silly. That is clowning. The joy experienced by real Christians is gladness. They are glad and thankful Jesus is preparing a permanent spiritual home in heaven for those who truly love Him and keep His commands. Real Christians are joyful when someone else chooses to follow Jesus. Real Christians are joyful when another person receives joy. Real Christians are joyful when they realize every challenge faced in the physical body is temporary, designed to prepare us spiritually to experience and be a part of the final joy, which is going to heaven.

> For the kingdom of God[19] is not a matter of eating and drinking but of righteousness and peace and joy in the Holy Spirit. (Romans 14:17)

The source of joy for real Christians is righteousness, peace, and joy in the Holy Spirit. The false source of joy for others is almost always something physical, such as unneeded possessions, fancy job titles, unlimited wealth, medals signifying high body counts in war, and anything man-made that pulls one's focus away from God.

A subset of joy is righteousness.

The concept of righteousness is not a common topic around the dinner table.

The short, superficial statement generally heard in the denominational world is, "Righteousness is 'being right' with God." It takes further study, especially of the Greek definitions, for the word to have real meaning in one's life.

The Greek word *dikaiosune* means (1) in a broad sense: state of him who is as he ought to be, righteousness, the condition acceptable to God; (1.a.) the doctrine concerning the way in which man may attain a state approved of God; (1.b.) integrity, virtue, purity of life, rightness, correctness of thinking feeling, and acting.

---

[19] The kingdom of God on earth is the worldwide collection of real Christians, His children.

The questions real Christians frequently ask themselves are, first, is my current state of being, my condition, acceptable to God? Second, if there are areas in my life where I need to improve, what am I doing to move closer to the state of being approved by God? Third, when God and others here on earth look at me, do they think of the words integrity, virtue, purity, rightness, correctness of thinking, feeling, and acting? If one can answer "yes," the one asking the questions can easily feel spiritual joy.

- *Those who actively demonstrate peace*

In the 1960s, the peace symbol spread across the world as war protesters marched against the Viet Nam and other wars. While not as popular today, the symbol can still be found, usually on signs and clothing worn by protesters. Many denominational Christians issue calls to pray for peace! There is only one flaw in their request: There will never be a physical peace, a national tranquility on the earth. On my desk, I have a calendar with a daily statistic. One reads, "The world has been at peace only 8 percent of the time over the last three thousand years." Real Christians can achieve personal, spiritual peace, but the purpose of Jesus coming to earth was not to bring an end to wars and conflicts between nations.

> Do not think that I have come to bring peace to the earth. I have not come to bring peace, but a sword. (Matthew 10:34)

The Greek word for peace is *eirene*: (1) a state of national tranquility; (1.a.) exemption from the rage and havoc of war; (2) peace between individuals—i.e., harmony, concord, security, safety, prosperity, felicity[20] (because peace and harmony make and keep things safe and prosperous); (4) of the Messiah's peace; (4.a.) the way that leads to peace (salvation); (5) of Christianity, the tranquil state of a soul assured of its salvation through Christ, and so fearing nothing from God and content with its earthly lot, of whatsoever sort that is; (6) the blessed state of devout and upright men after death.

The sword Jesus mentions is the Word of God. Every nation has those that can be defined as nationalists. Another term is "supporter of independence." Patriotism is similar, including terms like loyalist, flag waver, partisan, and xenophobia[21]. When one reads the account of Jesus's life, there is not one example of Him being interested in, or involved with, anything political. None!

From the time of Jesus until today, there have been hundreds of nations and governments, thousands of presidents, dictators, governors, mayors, and city council members. During the past, some have also claimed to be a god or the messiah. The only consistent, permanent, enduring, and lasting kingdom is real Christians who make up the family, the children of God.

---

[20] *Webster*: felicity: (1.a.) the quality or state of being happy especially great happiness; (b) an instance of happiness; (2) something that causes happiness

[21] *Xenophobia*: fear and hatred of strangers or foreigners or of anything that is strange or foreign.

Real Christians are focused on serving God, not an earthly nation or government leader. The weapon real Christians use is the Word of God.

> In all circumstances take up the shield of faith, with which you can extinguish all the flaming darts of the evil one; and take the helmet of salvation, and the sword of the Spirit, which is the word of God, praying at all times in the Spirit, with all prayer and supplication. To that end keep alert with all perseverance, making supplication for all the saints. (Ephesians 6:16–18)

> For the word of God is living and active, sharper than any two-edged sword, piercing to the division of soul and of spirit, of joints and of marrow, and discerning the thoughts and intentions of the heart. (Hebrews 4:12)

> Who shall separate us from the love of Christ? Shall tribulation, or distress, or persecution, or famine, or nakedness, or danger, or sword? As it is written, "For your sake we are being killed all the day long; we are regarded as sheep to be slaughtered." No, in all these things we are more than conquerors through him who

> loved us. For I am sure that neither death nor life, nor angels nor rulers, nor things present nor things to come, nor powers, nor height nor depth, nor anything else in all creation, will be able to separate us from the love of God in Christ Jesus our Lord. (Romans 8:35–39)

> So we do not lose heart. Though our outer self is wasting away, our inner self is being renewed day by day. For this light momentary affliction is preparing for us an eternal weight of glory beyond all comparison, as we look not to the things that are seen but to the things that are unseen. For the things that are seen are transient, but the things that are unseen are eternal. (2 Corinthians 4:16–18)

Real Christians have a deep, spiritual peace because they know there is nothing other people can do to cause them to not be loved by Jesus. This sense of peace is directly linked to joy also. In 2 Corinthians 4, we learn it is okay for our physical body to waste away. That is part of the natural journey we take. (See Ecclesiastes 12:1–7 and notice all the metaphors describing the aging process.)

Putting on peace means the real Christian will always have the God-given strength, when combined with patience, to turn away from anything that is tempting that person to deny Jesus. Then knowing they overcame the temptation, they will be at peace with themselves. Sleep tight!

- *Those who actively demonstrate patience*

We discussed patience in the "Think On" chapter. The difference here is going beyond thinking and acting so that others see our endurance, perseverance, and slowness in avenging wrongs (especially since vengeance belongs strictly to God).

> Repay no one evil for evil, but give thought to do what is honorable in the sight of all. If possible, so far as it depends on you, live peaceably with all. Beloved, never avenge yourselves, but leave it to the wrath of God, for it is written, "Vengeance is mine, I will repay, says the Lord." To the contrary, "if your enemy is hungry, feed him; if he is thirsty, give him something to drink; for by so doing you will heap burning coals on his head." [21] Do not be overcome by evil, but overcome evil with good. (Romans 12:17–21)

I want to make an observation about the phrase "heap burning coals on his head." This verse originally comes from Proverbs 25:21–22: "If your enemy is hungry, give him bread to eat, and if he is thirsty, give him water to drink, for you will heap burning coals on his head, and the Lord will reward you."

In Old and New Testament times, vendors wearing special coal-fired headgear walked through markets selling hot tea and coffee. Today, in Israel and Jordan for example, one can still buy hot coffee or tea from vendors wearing the same kind of special, coal-fired headgear. Some have incorrectly assumed that heaping hot coals on the head of one "serves them right!" for being the enemy. This verse must be read with verse 21 included. It does not make sense to give an enemy bread and water without providing a way to warm the bread and heat the water. A correct interpretation of this passage is, by bringing an enemy hot coals, they can now cook their food and make hot tea. They will also have hot coals, allowing them to build a fire in their own fireplace. Note the use of the word *heap*. This gift to an enemy is not a small amount of only a few coals but a heap—a pile! This is truly overcoming evil with good.

The Greek word for patience is *makrothumia*: (1) patience, endurance, constancy, steadfastness, perseverance; (2) patience, forbearance, longsuffering, slowness in avenging wrongs.

When it comes to being patient in one's actions, this passage from Romans 12 may be one of the most important for the real Christians to fully understand and identify with. First, the real Christian does not repay evil for evil. How often do we hear or read about pseudo-Christian patriots/nationalists who say, "Those foreign people kill Christians so we better kill them first!"

The real Christian knows all of humanity is foreign to this planet. Our spiritual souls were placed into this temporary body; and when the physical dies, the soul returns to God for judgment. Typically, "foreigner" means one not born in the country where the one who wants to kill them lives. Other terms include stranger, alien, and outsider. Wise, real Christians know these words also define them! We are foreigners, and our home is with God.

> So we are always of good courage. We know that while we are at home in the body we are away from the Lord, for we walk by faith, not by sight. Yes, we are of good courage, and we would rather be away from the body and at home with the Lord. So whether we are at home or away, we make it our aim to please him. For we must all appear before the judgment seat of Christ, so that each one may receive what is due for what he has done in the body, whether good or evil. (2 Corinthians 5:6–10)

Second, live peaceably with all, not just neighbors, not just those of the same ethnicity, not just those of the same religion., not just those of the same political party, not just those who speak the same language—*all!* The Greek word for "all" is actually two words: first, *pas*: (1) individually; (1.a.) each, every, any, all, the whole, everyone, all things, everything; (2) collectively; second, *anthropos*: (1.a.) human being, whether male or female; (1.a.) generically, to include all human individuals.

In other words, real Christians do all that is possible to be patient and live peaceably with all of humanity on the entire world! Being patient with others, and living in peace with them, does not include killing them! It includes feeding them, caring for them, teaching them, praying for and with them. It includes investing all the time needed to help them learn about God.

- *Those who actively demonstrate kindness*

The Greek word for kindness is *chrestotes*: (1) moral goodness, integrity; (2) benignity, kindness.

As with some of the other fruits, patience, when combined with love, can be a factor in showing kindness. If one is impatient, the result may be judging others unfairly. Without love, any kindness shown is superficial and wasted. If one is a chronic gossiper who condemns those who gossip, that person is also ignoring what it means to show kindness. A real Christian gives the other person every opportunity to accept kindness and continue to learn and grow in their faith. Notice the following passage. If God shows kindness in order for one to be led to repent, real Christians will do the same.

> Therefore you have no excuse, O man, every one of you who judges. For in passing judgment on another you condemn yourself, because you, the judge,

practice the very same things. We know that the judgment of God rightly falls on those who practice such things. Do you suppose, O man—you who judge those who practice such things and yet do them yourself—that you will escape the judgment of God? Or do you presume on the riches of his kindness and forbearance and patience, not knowing that God's kindness is meant to lead you to repentance? But because of your hard and impenitent heart you are storing up wrath for yourself on the day of wrath when God's righteous judgment will be revealed. (Romans 2:1–5)

We previously discussed kindness in the "Think On" chapter. As with patience, do more than think on. Act! Reread Romans 12:17–21 again and take time to realize how critical to one's spiritual survival this is.

● *Those who actively demonstrate goodness*

"Being good is not necessarily being godly. To be godly, though, is good. A sociology textbook in my library provides an example of goodness that is unrelated to godliness. The author describes the high level of cultural morality that is found among the Cheyenne, a group of Native Americans who once lived in Central Minnesota and Northern South Dakota. These people exhibited moderation, dignity, and

generosity and manifested an almost unbelievable degree of self-control. Parents loved their children and gave them a lot of affection without spoiling them. They also taught them ethical values at an early age so that many of them became dedicated, self-sacrificing, and well-behaved human beings. Yet these Indians were not Christians"[22] (italics in original copy).

Being good is nice. Those who own dogs are known to say something like, "Who's a good boy?" There is an excellent children's book by Margery Cuyler titled *That's Good! That's Bad!*[23] In the book, each page describes an event, and the result is either, "Oh, that's bad!" followed by, "No, that's good!" and vice versa. So what is good from a Christian point of view?

The Greek word for goodness is *agathosune*: uprightness of heart and life, kindness.

Some synonyms for uprightness are decency, honesty, and respectability. There is obvious overlap with kindness here. Real Christians are polite. They are courteous. They are well-mannered and respectful. They use goodness in action to recognize similarities instead of digging down to find differences.

> We share much more in common than we share in differences. (Bowen White, MD)

---

[22] Paul Lee Tan, *Encyclopedia of 7700 Illustrations: A Treasury of Illustrations, Anecdotes, Facts and Quotations for Pastors, Teachers and Christian Workers* (Garland TX: Bible Communications, 1996, c1979).

[23] ©1991 Henry Holt and Company, Inc. New York, New York.

Here are a few more verses talking about "good" and why it is an important fruit of the Spirit.

Being good is something that will be noticed on judgment day.

> His master said to him, "Well done, good and faithful servant. You have been faithful over a little; I will set you over much. Enter into the joy of your master." (Matthew 25:23)

The opposite of withhold is give!

> Do not withhold good from those to whom it is due, when it is in your power to do it. (Proverbs 3:27)

Real Christians do not grow tired from doing good things for others. Instead, they sleep well, physically tired and spiritually happy!

> And let us not grow weary of doing good, for in due season we will reap, if we do not give up. So then, as we have opportunity, let us do good to everyone, and especially to those who are of the household of faith. (Galatians 6:9–10)

It is a great gift to be acknowledged as being good.

> A good name is to be chosen rather than great riches, and favor is better than silver or gold. If there is nothing better than to be joyful and do good as long as we live, do it! (Proverbs 22:1)

> What gain has the worker from his toil? I have seen the business that God has given to the children of man to be busy with. He has made everything beautiful in its time. Also, he has put eternity into man's heart, yet so that he cannot find out what God has done from the beginning to the end. I perceived that there is nothing better for them than to be joyful and to do good as long as they live; also that everyone should eat and drink and take pleasure in all his toil—this is God's gift to man. (Ecclesiastes 3:9–13)

- *Those who actively demonstrate faithfulness*

Frequently, in the news, we hear of a dog owner who died and, after being buried, the faithful dog spent days lying by the headstone. There are other accounts of dogs waiting at a bus stop or train station platform because that was the last place they saw their owner. People in America, after attending a funeral, go on with their lives sometimes and may visit the grave of a loved one on Memorial Day.

The faithfulness of the Christian means so much more than a once-a-year visit in memory of someone who died. Earlier we discussed the weekly eating of the Lord's Supper to remember the entire life of Jesus. Eating the bread and drinking the wine is a faithful act. Faithfulness is more than "showing up." The faithfulness of real Christians grows over time because they understand what Matthew wrote:

> But the one who endures to the end will be saved. (Matthew 24:13)

The 1930 *Webster's Dictionary* defines endure as "to support without breaking or yielding; put up with; remain in; remain in the same state."

The same dictionary defines endurance as "the capacity to endure; power of suffering without succumbing; continuance; fortitude."

Some have said, "Life isn't fair." To real Christians, life is life. They accept that there will be days when everything goes well, and other days when life is challenging.

> For what credit is it if, when you sin and are beaten for it, you endure? But if when you do good and suffer for it you endure, this is a gracious thing in the sight of God. (1 Peter 2:20)

> But even if you should suffer for righteousness' sake, you will be blessed. (1 Peter 3:14a)

> Therefore let those who suffer according to God's will entrust their souls to a faithful Creator while doing good. (1 Peter 4:19)

Pseudo-Christians smile on Sunday then spend the rest of the week complaining about anything and everything that has absolutely nothing to do with their spiritual relationship with God. Examples include flat tires, sick kids, homeschooling because of the COVID-19, disagreeable coworkers, broken washing machines, a chipped tooth, utility bills, and on and on.

The suffering mentioned in three verses from 1 Peter are specific in nature.

First, in 1 Peter 2:20, suffering is when a Christian undergoes some kind of physical or emotional abuse as the result of doing something good. Second, in 1 Peter 3:14a, Christians are comforted, knowing even when they suffer for righteousness' sake, they will be blessed. Third, in 1 Peter 4:19, Christians who suffer do not spend time complaining. Instead, they give their souls to God and continue doing good. They remain faithful!

The Greek word for faithfulness is *pistis*: (1) conviction (certainty) of the truth of anything, belief; in the New Testament, of a conviction or belief respecting man's relationship to God and divine things, generally, with the included idea of trust and holy fervor (passion) born of faith and joined with it; (1.a.) relating to God; (1.a.1.) the conviction that God exists and is the creator and ruler of all things, the provider and bestower of eternal salvation through Christ; (1.b.) relating to Christ; (1.b.1.) a strong and welcome conviction or belief that Jesus is the Messiah through whom we obtain eternal salvation in the kingdom of God; (1.c.) the religious beliefs of Christians; (1.d.) belief with the predominate idea of trust (or confidence), whether in God or in Christ, springing from faith in the same; (2) fidelity, faithfulness; (2.a.) the character of one who can be relied on.

The last definition, in the Greek, is reliable. This is a multifaceted challenge and is identified by real Christians who are faithful to God. They are also true to the idea of wrapping everything we've covered so far into living every moment of every day on the quest to do the will of God as illustrated so well in the New Testament. And we still have two more topics to cover!

What actions can be seen by these real Christians? Their keeping one's word to friends and other Christians and humanity in general! Real Christians are consistent and can be counted on to do everything possible to help, teach, and be the example for others without excuse.

- *Those who actively demonstrate gentleness*

Many worldly people believe in war, armed responses, torture, all driven by hate, fear, and anger. They want to be stronger and more powerful than everyone else. Real

Christians have immense power under the love of Jesus, while worldly people want power over others. A simple, physical definition of gentleness came from a driver's education teacher. He said, "When pressing on the brakes for a routine stop, imagine you are pressing on an egg without breaking it. If it's a real emergency, break the egg!"

The Greek word for gentleness is *prautes*: mildness of disposition, gentleness of spirit, meekness.

Jesus showed gentleness to children as an example for us when showing gentleness to all people.

> And they were bringing children to him that he might touch them, and the disciples rebuked them. But when Jesus saw it, he was indignant and said to them, "Let the children come to me; do not hinder them, for to such belongs the kingdom of God. Truly, I say to you, whoever does not receive the kingdom of God like a child shall not enter it." And he took them in his arms and blessed them, laying his hands on them.[24] (Mark 10:13–16)

Read each of these synonyms for "gentle" and think about those who call themselves Christians. What words can you identify that describe those people?

Gentle means (1) free from all harshness, roughness, or intensity. Related words are: delicate, mellow, tender, hushed, low, soothing; calm, halcyon, peaceful, placid,

---

[24] Some view this not as a miraculous "laying on of hands" but simply gentle hugs.

quiet, serene, tranquil; (2) having a pleasant easygoing nature; kind, pleasant, pleasing, tender; agreeable, benign, mild; compassionate, kindly, softhearted, sympathetic, warmhearted. [25]

Take a few minutes to look up the antonyms (opposites) of all the positive, loving, and compassionate words listed above. The first question to ask is, "Do the Christians I know enthusiastically show these in their daily interactions with me and with others?" If these words do not describe one claiming to be a child of God, it is probably wise to look elsewhere for a real Christian who daily exhibit these actions and attitudes.

- *Those who actively demonstrate self-control*

Do you make excuses? "I didn't have the time." "My alarm didn't go off." "I only had enough money for donuts." "I forgot." "I was afraid I would make a mistake." "The power was off, and my garage door opener didn't work."[26]

Real Christians are self-disciplined and readily accept what God has given His children:

> for God gave us a spirit not of fear but of power and love and self-control. (2 Timothy 1:7)

---

[25] Inc *Merriam-Webster*, *Merriam-Webster's Collegiate Thesaurus*, Previously published as *Webster's Collegiate Thesaurus*. (Springfield, MA: *Merriam-Webster*, 1996, c1988).

[26] A true story. The individual's supervisor went to his house and showed him how to manually open the garage door!

The Greek word for self-control is *egkrateia*: the virtue of one who masters his desires and passions, especially his sensual appetites.

On average, at the time of this writing in 2019, the average bank credit card debt owed by Americans was $6,300. The old story of one who was called into his bank for writing a bad check comes to mind. When the man arrived, he said, "I still have plenty of checks in my checkbook. What's the problem?"

Real Christians master their desires and passions. They are not influenced by the barrage of advertising thrown at them throughout the day on television, radio, the Internet, etc. Real Christians are not fooled by the $19.95 price that almost miraculously fits every "must have," "new" invention being advertised for sale. (And "if you call now, get a second one absolutely free, shipping and handling fees are extra.")

Paul, in writing instructions to Timothy, a young Christian and a new leader of a congregation, spelled out the things Timothy would witness during his time with the assembly. As usual, Paul was honestly blunt!

> But understand this, that in the last days[27] there will come times of difficulty. For people will be lovers of self, lovers of money, proud, arrogant, abusive, disobedient to their parents, ungrateful, unholy,

---

[27] Last days refers to the time from the moment Jesus went back to heaven until the end of time. We are in the last days and have been for over two thousand years.

> heartless, unappeasable, slanderous, without self-control, brutal, not loving good, treacherous, reckless, swollen with conceit, lovers of pleasure rather than lovers of God, having the appearance of godliness, but denying its power. Avoid such people. (2 Timothy 3:1–5)

Again, we return to the three basic elements of human life: physical, emotional, and spiritual. Lack of physical self-control manifests itself in little to no physical exercise, overeating, eating and drinking unhealthy food and drink, and especially after retirement, sitting in front of the television for entire days at a time.

In 2015, nursing home residents watched television an average of between 45 and 77 percent every day.[28]

Lack of emotional self-control in adults results in outbursts of anger, yelling, hitting, kicking, throwing things, road rage, acts of revenge, and so many more.

The mindset seems to be, "I didn't get my way, and *you made me mad*, so I will do what I can to hurt you!" In both the physical and emotional negative reactions, the individual chooses their own response. No one person makes another person angry. Circumstances happen, and the individual on the receiving end is faced with a choice: be calm or be violent.

Some may say, "I can't control myself the way I should." Real Christians know God gives them the spirit of power and love and self-control. All one must do is open

---

[28] www.ncbi.nim.nih.gov, accessed June 18, 2019.

one's hands to let go of the useless, distracting physical and emotional things that interfere with the relationship with God, and take those now open hands and accept what he provides.

> Do not envy a man of violence and do not choose any of his ways, for the devious person is an abomination to the Lord, but the upright are in his confidence. (Proverbs 3:31–32)

Another tool to help identify real Christians is to spend some time thinking about the descriptive words found in 2 Timothy 3 and determine which of those who call themselves Christians routinely demonstrate these actions:

Lovers of self	Lovers of money	Proud (in an egotistical way)
Arrogant	Abusive (physically or emotionally)	
Ungrateful	Unholy	Heartless
Unappeasable	Slanderous	Without self-control
Brutal	Not loving good	Treacherous
Reckless	Swollen with conceit	Lovers of pleasure

Disobedient to their parents (i.e., adult "Christians" who do not care for elderly parents or do not listen to their loving advice on how to better live for Jesus)

Does anyone who claims to be a Christian come to mind? Notice the final warning of this passage: *Avoid them!*

It also may be time to look in the mirror for the same conduct!

Self-control is not punishment. It is self-discipline. It is strength of will and of mind. It exercises self-restraint. It is rewarding!

> Do you not know that in a race all the runners run, but only one receives the prize? So run that you may obtain it. Every athlete exercises self-control in all things. They do it to receive a perishable wreath, but we an imperishable. So I do not run aimlessly; I do not box as one beating the air. But I discipline my body and keep it under control, lest after preaching to others I myself should be disqualified. (1 Corinthians 9:24–27)

The "prize"? Eternal life with God in heaven.

Chapter 5 questions and challenges

1. Do these things: Choose to set the alarm clock. Choose to avoid hitting the snooze button. Choose to show up on time or maybe even a little early. Choose to eat healthy. Choose to exercise. Choose to study, pray, and relax. Choose to think before speaking or answering. Choose to develop profitable, beneficial habits.

2. Between where you are right now—physically, emotionally, and spiritually—and where you were when you first made a choice to do something good or bad, make a flowchart showing the results of both your good and bad decisions. Are you where you are now because of more good or bad decisions? What decisions are you facing right now? Where do you want your decisions to take you?

CHAPTER 6

Those Who...

No one has ever become poor by giving.

—Anne Frank

Some people have savings accounts and retirement funds. Some collect silver and gold. Some collect antiques. Some just never throw anything away! In 2018, the average donation by "Christians" was 2.5 percent of their incomes.[29] Some denominations expect a contribution of at least 10 percent of a member's income. This was called tithing in the Old Testament but is no longer required under the new covenant established by Jesus for real Christians.

- *Those who set aside money, food, clothing, etc. as part of a weekly planned budget so that the fruits of the Spirit can be actively demonstrated. This is not a part of the Lord's Day worship activities.*

---

[29] https://pushpay.com, accessed June 18, 2019.

The New Testament command on planned giving is very clear:

> Now concerning the collection for the saints: as I directed the congregations of Galatia, so you also are to do. On the first day of every week, each of you is to put something aside and store it up, as he may prosper, so that there will be no collecting when I come. And when I arrive, I will send those whom you accredit by letter to carry your gift to Jerusalem. If it seems advisable that I should go also, they will accompany me. (1 Corinthians 16:1–4)

When? Sunday. Where? Not specified. Who? "Each of you" (i.e., each individual). How much? "As he may prosper." (Other translations: "As God hath prospered him, that there be no gatherings when I come" [Authorized English version 1873]; "Every Sunday each of you must put aside some money, in proportion to what you have earned, and save it up, so that there will be no need to collect money when I come" [The Good News translation]; "On the first day of the week, each of you should set aside and save some of your money in proportion to what you have, so that no collections will have to be made when I come"[International Standard version]; "On the first day of every week, each one of you should set aside a sum of money in keeping with his income, saving it up, so that when I come no collections will have to be made" [New International version].)

Setting aside and budgeting a specified amount is a self-disciplined approach to giving. In many Christian households, the choice of how much to set aside frequently is made after all the regular bills are paid. While Old Testament laws are no longer in effect, the intent of one law can be a suggested guideline for one's giving.

> The Lord spoke to Moses, saying, "Speak to the people of Israel and say to them, When you come into the land to which I bring you and when you eat of the bread of the land, you shall present a contribution to the Lord. Of the first of your dough you shall present a loaf as a contribution; like a contribution from the threshing floor, so shall you present it. Some of the first of your dough you shall give to the Lord as a contribution throughout your generations. (Numbers 15:17–21)

Notice the use of the word *first*. The New Testament command is to set aside (give) an amount based on how one has been prospered or blessed by God.

Notice what the Scripture doesn't say: On the first day of every week, each of you is to put something aside and store it up, as he may prosper, after paying all your bills, figuring out how much cash you'll need for lunch money, and how much gas you'll need this week.

Real Christians set something aside as their first priority every week.

> Do your best to present yourself to God as one approved, a worker who has no need to be ashamed, rightly handling the word of truth. (2 Timothy 2:15)

Many congregations collect money during the official service, usually on Sunday morning. Typically done immediately following the communion, the one leading a prayer prior to the collection may say something like, "While not part of the communion, it is convenient that we take up the collection at this time." Then the same men who distributed the bread and wine now "pass the plates." The money is taken to another room where it is counted and then, usually, deposited in a local bank in the congregation's account. This can be a good thing or, sometimes, not so good.

The New Testament is very clear on how real Christians look at money.

> Do not lay up for yourselves treasures on earth, where moth and rust destroy and where thieves break in and steal, but lay up for yourselves treasures in heaven, where neither moth nor rust destroys and where thieves do not break in and steal.

For where your treasure is, there your heart will be also. The eye is the lamp of the body. So, if your eye is healthy, your whole body will be full of light, but if your eye is bad, your whole body will be full of darkness. If then the light in you is darkness, how great is the darkness! No one can serve two masters, for either he will hate the one and love the other, or he will be devoted to the one and despise the other. You cannot serve God and money. (Matthew 6:19–24)

And do not seek what you are to eat and what you are to drink, nor be worried. For all the nations of the world seek after these things, and your Father knows that you need them. Instead, seek his kingdom, and these things will be added to you. Fear not, little flock, for it is your Father's good pleasure to give you the kingdom. Sell your possessions, and give to the needy. Provide yourselves with moneybags that do not grow old, with a treasure in the heavens that does not fail, where no thief approaches and no moth destroys. For where your treasure is, there will your heart be also. (Luke 12:29–34)

One denominational congregation has close to $500,000 dollars in the bank, not being used, except to draw interest. There are probably others with much more.

Several years ago, a woman televangelist redecorated her house and spent over $261,000 dollars for sixty-eight pieces of furniture. That's over $3,800 per piece of furniture. $35,000 was used to redecorate the bathroom. So where is her treasure?

Where is the treasure of the congregation with half a million dollars sitting in the bank when there are hungry, lonely people only a few blocks away from the building?

There are several congregations of Christians in a European country who, on Mondays, following their congregational collection on Sunday, take the money and buy food and supplies for refugees and others in need. Every Monday. These congregations do not have a worship building. They rent a small space where they can meet because their homes are too small for very many to gather for worship.

The apostle Paul traveled all over the Middle East to spread the Word of God. On one journey, he was planning to stop by Corinth, pick up what had been set aside by the Christians there, and then take those gifts to help the poor Christians who were suffering in Jerusalem. This was no tithe as commanded in the Old Testament. Notice 1 Corinthians 16:2. Each person was to "put something aside" according to how much they had been prospered. In other words, if one was very rich, they would give a lot. If one was poor, they would give less. There was no set amount. Paul also said to put something aside. The word *something* in Greek means "who, which, what, or that." There is no specific command in this case to give only money. This could also include food, clothing, livestock, household items—anything that would help the struggling Christians in Jerusalem.

There are also no New Testament examples of a congregation's leadership (elders) taking anything and putting it in a savings account to draw interest. This command was given to individual Christians ("each of you" [v. 1]) to help as they could. Paul said that when he returned (possibly several years later), he would ensure the gifts went to Jerusalem.

For current times, it is up to individual Christians to look at their personal and family's physical resources: money, food, clothing, donatable items, time, anything that can be used to help other Christians and everyone else too.

> So then, as we have opportunity, let us do good to everyone, and especially to those who are of the household of faith. (Galatians 6:10)

Good can mean money. It can also mean helping a single mom buy medicine, clothes, or food. It can mean bringing new, warm socks to the elderly in a nursing home. It can mean anything that can be identified as "preplanned doing something good." Don't forget, both children and adults can be orphans!

> Religion that is pure and undefiled before God, the Father, is this: to visit orphans and widows in their affliction, and to keep oneself unstained from the world. (James 1:27)

The possibilities are endless. The rewards are eternal.

Chapter 6 questions and challenges

1. If you are a Christian, what can you do to expand your giving beyond a check or some cash tossed into the collection plate on Sunday?
2. How much "stuff" do you have in your home that has no emotional connection? Of the items hanging on your walls and sitting on tables, are there personal stories related to those things, or were they just "on sale" and everyone else was buying them too? Donate!

CONCLUDING THOUGHTS

In the introduction of this book, the following list was presented: war, murder, child abuse, trafficking of women and children, riots, terrorism, nationalism, starvation, greed, religious extremism, ego-power, rudeness, poverty, political and personal posturing, power-over, protests, homelessness, disease, earthquakes, global warming, drought, radical patriotism.

Critics of true Christianity falsely claim there is no God because, if there were, He wouldn't allow all these terrible things to exist. They claim that if God was real, Christians could fix all these problems. Critics claim this Christian nation (the United States) proves religion is useless and ineffective. In a sense, the critics are partially correct because there is no such thing as an earthly "Christian" nation.[30] In the Old Testament, God rewarded and punished both individuals and nations. Under the new covenant of Jesus, God deals with individuals, not with nations.

The causes of all the problems listed above are not because God doesn't exist but because of humans who've chosen lives of sin and ignorance instead of the traits and

---

[30] See the list of recommended books in Appendix 1.

actions of real Christians presented in this book. Luke, in recording the words of Peter, wrote:

> So Peter opened his mouth and said: "Truly I understand that God shows no partiality, but in every nation anyone who fears him and does what is right is acceptable to him. (Acts 10:34–35)

Peter used the words *every nation*, then the word *anyone*. "Every" means *all*, the entire world! The second part of verse 35 is so important for the one trying to find real Christians. They will be those who fear God and do what is right from His point of view. The Greek word for fear is *phobeo*: reverence (respect), venerate (adore; worship), to treat with deference (high esteem) or reverential (respectful) obedience. ("And his mercy is for those who respect him from generation to generation" [Luke 1:50].)

Doing what is right includes everything mentioned in this book. Real Christians are those who anyone can easily see the respect, adoration, high esteem, and respectful obedience of God in their daily lives. Real Christians need God and are willing to allow Him to comfort them, hear their prayers, and provide blessings to satisfy their physical, emotional, and spiritual needs. The Word of God is like medicine for the Christian's soul. The model for giving medications can be customized to how real Christians handle their daily interactions with all others. Both physical medicine and the "spiritual and emotional medicine" of the Word of God must be given according to the following rules:

- the correct medicine
- in the correct amount
- to the correct person
- at the correct time
- by the correct method
- with the correct attitude

The one who chooses to become a Christian chooses to worship God, chooses to think about what it means to be a Christian, chooses to put on the spiritual garments of a Christian, chooses to demonstrate the fruits of the Spirit, and chooses to give generously of themselves and all they have, can now look in the mirror and see the real Christian!

Peter provided a perfect summation of the real Christians life:

> His divine power has granted to us all things that pertain to life and godliness, through the knowledge of him who called us to his own glory and excellence, by which he has granted to us his precious and very great promises, so that through them you may become partakers of the divine nature, having escaped from the corruption that is in the world because of sinful desire. For this very reason, make every effort to supplement your faith with

virtue, and virtue with knowledge, and knowledge with self-control, and self-control with steadfastness, and steadfastness with godliness, and godliness with brotherly affection, and brotherly affection with love. For if these qualities are yours and are increasing, they keep you from being ineffective or unfruitful in the knowledge of our Lord Jesus Christ. For whoever lacks these qualities is so nearsighted that he is blind, having forgotten that he was cleansed from his former sins. Therefore, brothers, be all the more diligent to make your calling and election sure, for if you practice these qualities you will never fall. For in this way there will be richly provided for you an entrance into the eternal kingdom of our Lord and Savior Jesus Christ. (2 Peter 1:3–11)

APPENDIX 1

RECOMMENDED READING LIST

1. ~~God~~ Greed Bless America?: God Never Will Bless America
    ©2012 Joseph Alan Redman. Tate Publishing, LLC. (Note: Book is out of print but may be available from used book stores.)
2. *The Devils' Door: The Cult of the Dead*
    ©2017 Keith Sisman. Forbidden Books, United Kingdom
3. *The Myth of a Christian Nation: How The Quest for Political Power Is Destroying the Church*
    ©2005 Gregory A. Boyd. Zondervan, Grand Rapids, Michigan 49530
4. *The End of White Christian America*
    ©2016 Robert P. Jones. Simon and Schuster, 1230 Avenue of the Americas, New York, NY 10020

5. *The Search for Christian America*
   ©1989 Mark A. Noll, George M. Marsden, and Nathan O. Hatch. Helmers & Howard Publishers, Inc. P.O. Box 7407, Colorado Springs, CO 80933 USA
6. *Traces of the Kingdom*
   ©2010 Keith Sisman. Forbidden Books, P.O. Box 1, Huntington, PE262YZ, United Kingdom
7. *Unchristian America: Living with Faith in a Nation that Was Never under God*
   ©2008 Michael A. Babcock. SALTRIVER® Tyndale House Publishers, Inc.

ABOUT THE AUTHOR

Joseph Redman is a strong believer in the Bible and the one true living God. He became a Christian in 1959. Raised as an army brat, he worshipped here in the USA, in Japan, and in (West) Germany. He is an army veteran who served as a helicopter ambulance medic in (South) Việt Nam. He is a folk singer in nursing homes, a humanitarian clown, a husband, father, grandfather, and a food bank volunteer. He believes the true simplicity of being a real Christian is found only in the New Testament.

Printed in the USA
CPSIA information can be obtained
at www.ICGtesting.com
LVHW091919170724
785217LV00001B/58